Drones & Drone… gy
on Un… l
Ve…

by

Geoff Parsons

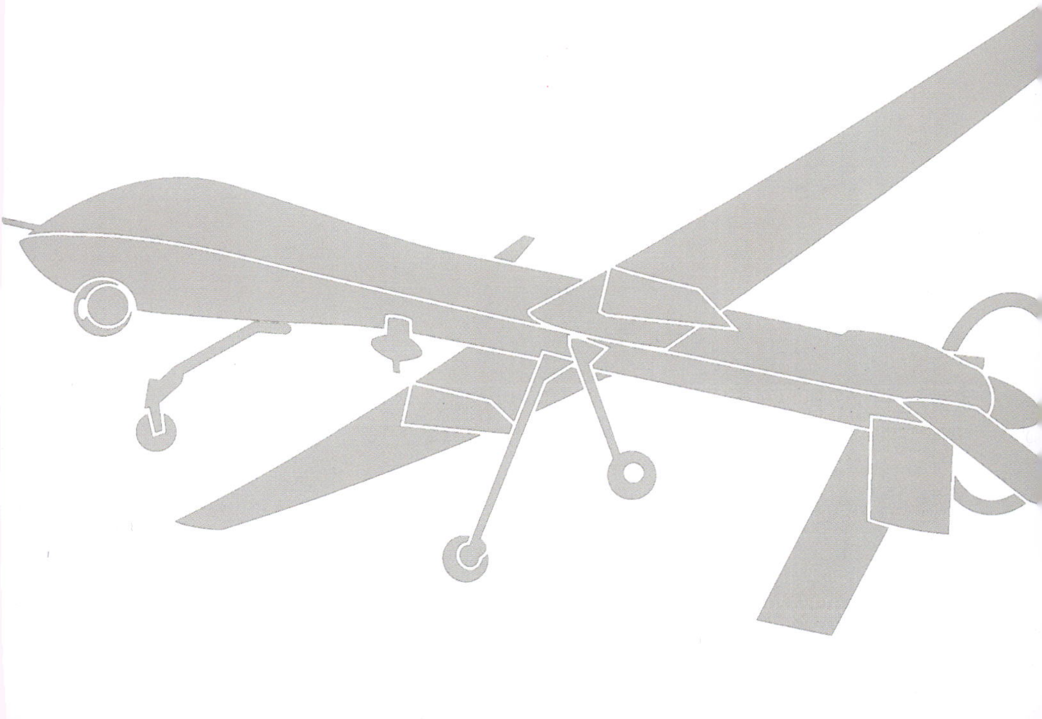

Published by **Jaefoo Books Publishing**

Drones & Droneology on Unmanned Aerial Vehicle Systems

ISBN 978-0-9955296-0-1

First published in Great Britain in 2016 by Jaefoo Books Publishing.

Cover illustration by Graham Parfitt, Designbox Studio Limited. Set by Graham Parfitt and printed in the United Kingdom.

Contents

Author's Note

Shortly after starting earlier this year I realised that I had never twigged that drone technology has been around for decades. A drone was found in my town and I became interested that the owner could not be traced. WHY...?

The interest expanded when I realised that unmanned aerial vehicle systems are now increasingly being taken seriously for a multitude of commercial, military and recreational tasks by businesses, government agencies, local government, and other public service bodies; and, of course, by individuals. Hence this book!

Now the drone is being used, or at least tested, in many situations I thought it opportune to see, briefly in each instance, what is being done with unmanned aerial vehicles systems (UAVSs) otherwise known, perhaps more commonly as drones. Once I started I found a paucity of definitions which gave me clarity of meanings of the new words I was coming upon – hence the definitions given in italics in Part 2.

Parts

The book is in nine parts:

Part 1 **Flying Drones within the Law**
Part 2 **Definitions, Descriptions and Explanations**
Part 3 **Abbreviations and Acronyms**
Part 4 **Categories of Terms**
Part 5 **Bibliography and References**
Part 6 **Directory of Organisations.**
Part 7 **List of Tables**
Part 8 **Index of Countries**
Part 9 **Timeline of Droneology**

Errors and Omissions

I have endeavoured to confirm details of my entries by reference to the bibliography and a multitude of library books, magazines, and other resources, eg online blogs, web-conference recordings. As stated above friends have kindly read parts of the text and commented on points where the text was uncertain or confused! Nevertheless, I cannot claim infallibility and ask that you let me know of the errors that you may find – few, I hope! I am responsible for any errors; likewise omissions.

Warning!

Furthermore I ask the following:

- Please bear in mind that droneology is a fast moving subject and changes occur frequently.
- Please do not rely on any entry when making decisions of a commercial or personal nature - in this respect it is often important to obtain professional advice.

How to Use this Book

1 Your reading on aerial drones may give you a term which you may not know well, or even not at all. You should find a clear definition in the text of Part 2.

2 Having seen the definition you may want to go further. To help you some Part 2 entries are cross referenced to other like definitions or an explanation or expansion of the topic. On the other hand, some are contrasting!

3 You may come upon or hear elsewhere of

say, a drone-related topic or organisation which is new to you. If so you may find a brief explanation or description of it in Part 2 or Part 6.

4 Part 3 gives the abbreviations and acronyms used. Please bear in mind that Part 3 includes a few entries which I have found in sources but not used in the book elsewhere.

5 Having touched upon a topic in a textbook, film, etc, you may wish to expand upon it. Part 4 should list a generic category by name or word which I hope fits your topic in some way. You should find that the cluster of terms helpful. A reading of the listed terms in a selected category should then increase your overall understanding.

Finale on Potential Career Development

I really hope that you will find the book, despite potential inadequacies, a source of inspiration to get into droneology, perhaps as:

- a commercial drone pilot,
- a drone designer,
- a dronelaw-maker,
- a drone-based systems integrator...............

....

...................the field appears to have limitless expansion.
If not for a career, becoming a hobbyist or drone racer will be exciting and... ...who knows?

Acknowledgements

A book of this nature relies on numerous sources from which to gather cognate material.

My principal sources are given in the Bibliography and References. Similarly, I have found the World Wide Web an invaluable common for gleaning seeds of interest and the nutrients to grow them into entries.

In particular I have found the official websites of organisations are a must to obtain details of particular issues and concerns (see Part 6). In this respect I would acknowledge with thanks the permission of the following:

- *Parish Council of Bishopstoke* - to quote from the parish's byelaws where they refer to drones, and
- *Property Drone Consortium* - to quote from the organisation's website.

I must thank several who have read a part of the text and commented upon it. They are *Roger Bryan*, *Ray Craddock*, *Mark Fittock*, *Carla*, *June*, *Sophie* and *Simon Parsons*, and *Alan Proto* – in particular Mark's comments on early full text induced many improvements and additions: as well as removal of some gaffes! Finally, *Graham Parfitt's* invaluable help and advice on the graphics and imagery have immensely improved the book.

Flying Drones within the Law

Commercial Pilots

The tables on pages 1 to 4 give points about flying UVASs in the UK and USA respectively. They are not intended as a statement of the law but an aide memoire of what a drone pilot or manager needs to be aware. Commercial UAV pilots and business managers will, no doubt, know them or have been busily absorbing the just announced FAA's regime changes applicable from 29 August, 2016 in the USA. In the UK will have started thinking about the implications of the outcome of Brexit and the CAA's IN - 2016/073.

Public Service Pilots

Police officers, university staff and other public service officials who are pilots of UAVSs are treated as follows:

1. UK In brief, they would need a drone pilot qualification, insurance, etc but the CAA's PFAW or equivalent would be unnecessary.
2. USA In brief a) they may take the Part 107 route like commercial pilots, or b) recognising limitations, obtain the equivalent of public Certificate or Authorisation (COA) and possibly an emergency COA (e-COA).

UK

The CAA's rules for UVASs are given in the Air Navigation Order 2016 particularly Articles 240, 241, 94 and 95. They must be observed by pilots and/or managers of drone businesses and public services in the UK from 25 August, 2016. On the Brexit decision – the European and UK airspace regulatory authorities have been progressing joint work on changes to the UAV airspace regime with the intent to amalgamate it with manned aviation rules, etc. Brexit may weaken the impact of UK suggestions, etc but hopefully concurrent work towards an agreed pan-Europe UAVS regime is virtually complete..? Finally, Kent Police and others are working with EU counterparts to improve border security. Brexit implications will need to be addressed..?

Pointers to Good Flights and to the CAA Rules for Commercial UAVSs (UK)

Safety, etc

- Fly safely – not recklessly, not negligently ... etc – so as to avoid: a) injury to persons, b) disrespect of a person's privacy, and c) damage to their property (see Article 241). A look at Articles 240, 241, 94 and 95 will give wider precise details of the law on this area.
- Be alert and rested (not tired), without alcohol and drugs.
- Give way to other aircraft and observe airspace restrictions – essentially for the purposes of airspace safety, national security, ...etc (see Article 240).
- Monitor changes to the UAV flying rules which may be introduced by the CAA at any time, eg because of a) the forthcoming strategy, and b) the decision for the UK to leave the EU.

Aircraft

- Ensure the UAV is airworthy with the appropriate official and in-house paperwork for modification, repair, maintenance...etc for the types of work and areas of operation
- Registration of drones is not yet required in the UK – but monitor

Pilot

- Hold the appropriate CAA-approved commercial UAV pilot's qualifications for the proposed drone and work from a NQE – BNUC or BNUC-S and, possibly an award for a specialist kind of flying
- Hold a PFAW or equivalent before commencing any flying for remuneration
- Ensure operational manual, logbook is in order and maintained as appropriate
- As pilot in control ensure the operator of the controls in competent and brief him or her as appropriate

Insurance

- Hold the appropriate insurance cover - the drone, cargo, pilot, employees, public liability,... etc
- Know the terms and conditions of the policy and comply with them at all times – keeping appropriate records, etc – logbook, notifications of incidents...etc.

Work Procedures

- Engage with the various law-based, industry-based or work-based protocols on: education and training, emergency and rescue, health and safety, privacy and surveillance ...etc.
- Be aware of the possibility of restrictions to flying due to a) local authority byelaws, b) another body's byelaws and c) other land rights (see Part 2).

Pre-flight

- Before any flight, ensure wareness of weather conditions which may adversely affect the flight...etc – take reasonable precautions or abort the mission
- Before any flight carry out a pre-flight check and prepare the UAV for a safe flight
- Prepare a flight plan and notify any authority as appropriate...etc – air traffic control, Royal Navy (in Cornwall, for instance)
- Ensure the cargo's payload is within weight and size limits and contains no prohibited goods... etc. ● Do not fly from ground vehicles, etc.

Flying

- Do not fly beyond the line-of-sight - which taken to be say, 500 metres
- Do not fly above 400 feet from the ground – the space above is for manned aircraft
- Do not fly over crowds and do not fly at night – local time
- Do not fly within 50 metres of buildings or structures, individuals, etc, vehicles
- Do not fly with first-person-vision, ect - unless lawfully organised
- Know and observe any distance restrictions so as to keep away from airports and other specified areas - infrastructure, prisons, stadia, etc.
- Photography is particularly strict for surveillance purposes with prescribed distances in given situations ● If with camera, respect privacy, national security etc.

USA

On 21 June 2016 the FAA announced that the rules for flying small drones were to change. The new ones operate from 29 August 2016. They must be observed by pilots and/or managers of small-UAV businesses in the USA. Many of the more general rules given for the UK are not included in the box below – they may be of interest. Please note that most of the points raised in the box on page 1 will apply in the USA but some may have variations in detail.

Pointers to Good Flights and to the FAA Rules (new Part 107) for Commercial UAVSs (USA)

Pilot

- A remote pilot is in command and control the UAV
- Usually he or she will be able to fly unaided as pilot in command (PIC) but the PIC may be in charge of another who is operator of controls
- Fly only if you are at least 16 years of age, qualified and competent
- Foreign accredited qualifications are not yet recognised in the USA – so pilots qualified overseas will need to obtain a FAA recognised certificate

UVAS

- These rules apply to drones under 55lbs (24.9kg)
- Airworthiness certification is not required of small drones but the pilot should be able to show observance of pre-flight check protocols (written up)

Flying

- Do not fly above 400 feet from the ground – the space above is for manned aircraft
- Do not fly beyond the line-of-sight
- Know and observe any distance restrictions so as to keep away from airports and other specified areas, infrastructure, etc
- Do not fly over crowds
- Do not fly at night-time
- If flying at dusk, use appropriate lights

As in the UK, state legislation and local law, etc may affect the flying of drones. Pilots and managers need to be aware that jurisdictional conflict may arise between Federal law and local law regimes – it is understood that the former prevail.

Hobbyist, Recreational and Racing Drone Flyer

The hobbyist, etc seems to be relatively lightly treated under the rules in the UK and the USA - but the penalties may not be lighter! So the hobbyist may have a lighter letter of the law (but not really), so he or she needs to embrace the code of safe flying as does the professional pilot. With this in mind, the box sets out rules from both the UK and USA. (Other countries may have some rule, protocol, etc which may be better.) In other words, the box below is the result of seeking best practice from the domains of drones, recreation and management.

Amalgam of Tips and Flying Rules
Non-professional Drone Flyer

Law

- Know you country's Dronecode of law inside out, eg register, if needed

Education and Training

- Seek and undertake early training and self-improvement – perhaps even enough to attain professional status in due course ● Learn your handling, eg of controls, on a simulator and/or a very inexpensive drone ● Do no paid work unless qualified

Insurances

- Take out third party insurance – perhaps joining a club which offers that and more insurance cover

Pre-flight preparations

- Consider the need for protective clothing and propeller guards, etc ● Other than in a genuine emergency, obtain the property owner's permission to fly whilst on their land - See page 13 Byelaws
- Transport a) drone safely in protective case with uninstalled batteries, and b) carry LiPo batteries separately in secure /safe case ● Develop habits leading to good flying and an airworthy drone- weather check, pre-flight checks,risk assessment at the ground base

Modifications, Repairs and Maintenance

- On procurement of a drone check for any warranty etc and comply with it for better success in claim
- Carryout in accord with the manufacturer's advice any necessary modifications, repairs and maintenance to your drone before attempting to fly it. Carryout pre-flight checks and make good

Flying

- Observe your country's airspace height and visual distance limitations ● Do not fly from vehicles
- Know of and observe any local national drone-no-go restrictions – military bases, airports, power stations, prisons, sports stadia, etc ● Keep say 50 metres from buildings and people etc.
- Fly only if you are competent and do so safely, not endangering others and with respect for others – no injury to them, no damage to their property and no loss to their privacy. So avoid collisions with other aircraft. ● Do not fly over any settlements
- Do not fly beyond the line-of-sight - 500 metres, but check. Do not fly at night.
- Do not fly over crowds, eg in a sports stadium ● Do not fly FPV unless in lawful event

A

Definitions, Descriptions and Explanations

accelerometer

A sensor which detects linear movement in three dimensional straight line directions.
Cf see page 39 ***gyroscope***

Advantages of working with drones

Work with drones has advantages which are pushing the boundaries of applications to agriculture, construction industry, property and facilities, real estate and many other service sectors. Commentators cite the following drivers to saving time and money as well as enhanced outcomes:

- cost reduction due to ease of working and nature of capital equipment
- cost of capital equipment is reduced
- data outcomes are improved in terms of real time collection and quality and quantum of data
- data analysis in terms of time taken for collection and analytical results
- health and safety of staff in harsh or hazardous environments or contexts, eg radiation from nuclear power station failure
- imagery outcomes – because of increased quantity and quality, and reduced costs
- data outcomes are improved in the amount of data collected
- time saving.

See page 59 **Military advantages for UAVSs**

aerial droneology / droneology

The study of unmanned aerial vehicles (UAVs), unmanned aerial vehicle systems (UAVSs), and cognate aspects of their associated technologies together with their organisational and situational environments.

Aerial filming and photography with a drone

Professional filming and photography with a drone is a specialised and this item merely hints at aspects as an aide memoire. The following points are given:

- most countries have privacy laws and specific regulatory requirements which must be observed when flying drones and for filming and photography work
- clients who use a drone filming and photography business are likely to want prior evidence of previous work and how a job is conducted
- a drone's flight battery life is normally about 20 minutes but might be less than half that when loaded with equipment.

aerial tanker drone

For refuelling airborne fighter aircraft, an UAVS which carries fuel from any USN aircraft carriers which have an installed UAV command centre, eg USS Carl Vinson.

Agricultural industry and drones

1. Dropping articles for the purposes of agriculture is covered by Article 91 of ANO 2016. It requires a) an aerial application certificate and b) an aerial application manual.

2. The use of drones in agriculture has grown in recent years as new applications of drone technologies have been designed and deployed world-wide. Such agricultural uses of drones include:

• land surveying and plan making • identifying areas lacking in certain nutrients • spraying land with fertilisers • crop monitoring for diseases and pests • rounding up sheep • searching for lost sheep • spraying to combat disease and pests • estimating crop yields • eradication of weeds.

In short, drones allow so-called "precision agriculture" in that, for example, using pesticides may be used more exactly - when and where needed.

Aid

See page 78 **"Regulation" for aid**

Air

A mix of gases which comprises carbon dioxide, nitrogen, and oxygen; and carries other gases, fumes, particulates and vapours, eg water vapour, for instance, as clouds.
Air might be regarded as a common, available to all and essential for sustaining life.

Air and sea drone

An air and submersible sea drone has been developed by Oakland University. Uses are likely to include:

- law enforcement – border patrol, smuggling and fishing
- pipeline inspections
- search and rescue.

Aircraft – meaning applied to drones

1. USA In terms of statute law in the USA, a drone is an aircraft, albeit unmanned and remotely piloted. It must therefore comply with aviation law. Nevertheless, the FAA document - *Law enforcement guidance for suspected unauthorised UAS operations* - sets out three broad points about drones:
1) law and drones as aircraft
2) law and drones as recreational or hobby vehicles
3) law and drones in terms adopting non-recreational flying and other aspects.

2. UK The principal legislation is the series of Civil Aviation Acts up to 2012. Under the legislation the Civil Aviation Authority (CAA) is the body primarily developing dronelaw and practice, eg with the Air Navigation Order 2016 (see immediately below). Dronelaw and practice is being developed and a 10 year national strategy is expected later in 2016. See page 4 **aerial droneology/droneology**

Air Navigation Order 2016 (ANO)

The ANO is a statutory document enacted in 2016 which regulates the use of drones of 150kg or less in the UK.
It is administered by the Civil Aviation Authority and came into operation on 25 August, 2016.

Airports and drone threats

It is expected that a considerable staff cost saving will be achieved as an outcome from drone trials conducted by the National Counter Terrorism Policing Headquarters at Gatwick airport.

The police will deploy drones at Heathrow, Luton and Stanstead and other airports to defend against intruders using drones and other means

Airspace - law

1. **Common Law and airspace** - In common law, briefly, the landowner owns and holds the freehold estate from the centre of the earth to the heights of the heavens. In other words, the landowner owns the airspace above the surface of the land and, for the record, any voids ("airspace") beneath the surface: for practical purposes, however, outer space is outside of the concept except where mentioned in this book. Ownership of the ordinary airspace is subject to four other general matters, namely:

1) any leases, tenancies, licences, grants, etc the landowner grants or makes to others
2) any statutory law – Acts, statutory instruments and other secondary legislation - enacted for administrative and other public purposes by parliament and authorised bodies, eg local authority byelaws.
3) any law pertaining to aviation and other matters, such as general international agreements, bi-lateral and multi-lateral agreements, conventions, treaties and the like between countries
4) any relevant military law, such as a) rules of engagement, b) rules for the use of force and c) rules of war which embody aspects of human and other rights.

2. **Statutory law** – For flying, the UK's airspace is controlled or regulated by the national Civil Aviation Authority (CAA), subject to any international aviation, etc law adopted by the government.
For drone pilots the authority is likely to have developed 'columns' or 'volumes' of controlled or restricted airspace within which flying is prohibited or otherwise.

Airspace - law (continued)

3. **International and European aviation law** – Manned aviation between countries is governed by international laws and/or European law. Such law is not wholly developed for drones but in Europe moves are tending to a pan-European system of legal controls. In the UK such law will be managed and administered by the CAA.

As far as is known there is no international consensus on the 'volumes' or 'columns' mentioned above – although there are commonalities. As regulatory regimes develop commonalities are likely to be increasingly used and developed. It is conceivable that as cross-border drone flying develops, eg drone deliveries, increased international cooperation will come about.

Air traffic control systems for drones

A number of approaches to creating a system of air traffic control are being investigated and trialled.
The table shows some approaches to the development of systems.

Air traffic control systems for drones	
Technology	**Approach**
Internet-based system	• Initially, by way of submitting flight plans to an air traffic control centre • Latter uses a) real time data about the weather, b) other UAV traffic and c) hazards along the proposed route • Accordingly, consent is given, the route is amended or denied.
Mobile or cellphone based system	• The features of such a system would need to cover the following: • Provide extensive connectivity though an Internet of Things (IoT) development • Has cloud technology to permanently store collected data • Holds details of each drone on the system • Provides an electronic logbook for all flights • Automatically uploads details of any flight • Has radar technology to alert you of nearby drones, etc • Provides a secure system. *My RPATS* is an existing app which provides for cloud records of flights. It is based on technologies like a) Android technology, b) a cloud storage, and c) GPS.

Airworthiness 1

EU EUROUC International have developed standards for accreditation and approvals of a) airworthiness, b) design and production, c) flight crew licencing d) flight schools, e) light UAS scheme, and f) manufacturer's procedures and production.

Airworthiness 2

UK 1. ANN One of more than 30,000 documents on a CAA database of AANs. They are in effect an approval of airworthiness at a given time and in this book apply to large UAVs.

2. Issue(s) The first issue may be corrected or changed in some minor way to improve it, eg typos. When published "Issue 2"describes it accordingly. Any other such issues follow in numbered sequence.

3. Addendum When an ANN is changed in substance in some relatively important way it is by an "Addendum" to the latest Issue.

---

almost ready to fly (ARF)

A drone which is not yet fully built and may have one or more missing essential parts.

See page 75 **ready to fly (RTF)**

Ambulance drone

An ambulance UAVS is one specially designed to carry either service casualties or civilians who are injured or sick. Possible applications in relatively dangerous environments where the human pilot would be at risk include: a) battlefield, b) a combat zone with insurgents, c) an area contaminated by nuclear radiation, eg from a power station failure, a dirty bomb.

Two instances of ambulance drone are known:

1 Trials are in hand in Israel with a drone, Cormorant (was AirMule), to pick up battlefield casualties or injured evacuees from a natural disaster area – hopefully by 2020, and

2 "Drone Ambulance" so-called carries a defibrillator to individuals in cardiac arrest. Expected to be available in 2019, this Netherlands drone would enable a 'man in the street' to administer the defibrillator under the guidance of a remotely situated doctor.

Analogue technology

A technology used, for instance, in drone video work where the absence of latency may be important, eg racing drones. It transmits at a frequency of 5.8GHz.

Cf page 91 **WiFi**

Anti-drone measures

The table gives examples of anti-drone measures.

Anti-drone measures	
Device or system	**Comment**
Acoustic sensor	• Tend to be adversely affected by local ambient noise • Generally not suitable in noisy , eg urban places • Require a frequently updated database of the noise signature of each drone
Anti-Defence System (AUDS)	• Detects at 10km • Tracks the flight path • Inhibits the radio signals to stop control, etc. • Defeat with a device
Geofences	• virtual barrier around a building, estate or facility • it is used to detect an approaching airborne drone See page 37 **Geofence**
Jamming	• a device which emits signals to mask the control signals used by the operator • then used to bring down the drone See 46 **Jamming**
Laser beam	• US Army has a high energy laser mobile test truck (HELMTT) • Sends a 10 kW laser beam at an intrusive drone to burn it up
Net drone	• a drone carrying a net which is shot at an 'enemy' drone to capture it in flight
Raptors	• raptors trained to capture drones whilst flying • eagles and falcons have been trained
Spoofing	• an over-ride device • used to take control of an airborne drone and fly it or cause it to crash See page 84 **Spoofing**.

auto redaction
In surveillance, the process of recording by camera where certain imagery is not taken or faces etc are obscured, eg by misting out.

autonomous flying
A mode of flying where the drone is not directly controlled by a pilot but is most usually guided by pre-set flight parameters given to or determined by the pilot.
In line-of-sight flying a drone which leaves the line of sight will usually have pre-set autonomous instructions to return to land.

Sometimes, however, another person may take-over the drone or some other intervention will affect the flight of a drone. Examples include:
1. an external agent who is jamming and spoofing the drone
2. the parameters of a geofence
3. the parameters of segregated airspace, eg a blue line corridor or red line corridor.
4. a flight tutor with an override controller.

barrel roll
Rotation around the longitudinal axis of a drone when it is flying.

barometric pressure sensor
A sensor which is used in an altimeter to measure height above ground level.

Battery (1)

B

An on-board battery is the drone's source of power for the motors, etc.
A common battery with say three cells (3s) and 1500 mAh will give up to about 20 minutes flying time for a typical quadcopter – so a pilot will carry say, a dozen spares.
The principal characteristics of a battery for a drone are the number of cells (s) and the power measured in milli amp hours (mAh).

Battery (2)
One or more portable backpacks are available to use in other situations, eg the DroneDefender, a drone detector and capture device, is powered in this way.

battery eliminator circuit
A way of using the main battery to power both the motors of the drone and other components which require, in fact, less power.

B4UFLY app
The FAA's B4UFLY app which warns drone operators with information, eg interactive maps and data of any no-drone zones and other restrictions, etc which are currently applicable in the vicinity of a current or proposed flying place.

bind
The communications connection between the controller and the drone.

binding
The action of making the communications connection between the controller and the drone.

BNUC and BNUC-S

Two basic European level global UAV qualifications are recognised by the CAA, for commercial pilots seeking authorisation to fly, namely:

1. Basic National UAV Certificate for UAVs of less than 150kg
2. Basic National UAV Certificate-S for UAVs of less than 20kg.

Both involve two parts: 1) a taught theory course and theory examination, and 2) a operations manual assessment and a flight operations examination.

They are not yet recognised by ther FAA.
In addition, a relatively new scheme involves an application for the recognition of the applicant's existing qualification and experience, eg as a pilot of manned aircraft.
(Finally, it may be noted the above skims the range of qualifications, approaches to seeking permission to fly, etc.)

Bird counting

Trials with a drone carrying a camera has been used from a boat at sea to count seabirds nesting on cliffs. If successful it should prove more efficacious than counting with binoculars.
A freeze framing technique is used in the back office to count the birds.

bladder tank

A liquid fuel tank for drones which comes in many forms so as to be fitted into, for instance, the fuselage, nacelle or wing.

blue line corridor

A blue line corridor is a proposed designated route for large commercial cargo drone route, often in and around cities, eg in Africa.

body

The core of the drone to which other components are attached and interconnected. (It is likely to be enclosed by the case.)

booms

Bracket-like components which protrudes horizontally, etc. from the body of a drone; each of which carries a motor and rotor.

brain controlled interface (BCI)

Brain controlled interface is a technology which uses electrical activity of the human brain to control a drone through a electroencephalogram headset which is programmed to use particular thoughts coded as algorithms for guiding the UAV.
Drone races have been tried in Florida to test BCI.

Brexit decision

See page 51 **Law and drones**
See page 52 **Legislation, etc on drones**

"build"	A colloquial term used as a noun by the builder of a do-it-yourself drone when referring to the drone he or she built.
Building and structure inspections	Surveys of roofs and the walls of high buildings are frequently undertaken by drone carried cameras. In such situations ladders, scaffolding, slings and the like are unnecessary. Thus drone inspections offer a health and safety advantage. In the UK if either a contractor is employed by the building owner or the work is done in-house, the pilot must be qualified under CAA regulations and flight plan and other operational requirements are met in law. Examples of work which may be undertaken include: ● blocked guttering on facades and roof gullies and gullies, etc behind parapets ● damage to the building structure and roof ● decorative condition ● energy leakages ● detecting rust on ironworks ● heat leakages (using thermal imaging – particularly at night) ● steam leakages (using thermal imaging – particularly at night) ● water leakages.
Business approvals or exemptions	By mid-April 2016 the AUVSI reported that the FAA had approved many drone businesses under the section 333 exemption of the FAA Modernization and Reform Act 2012 (FMRA). The growth rate is seemingly several hundred a month. Some 38 types of mainly small business units have been categorised as approved, including: ● aerial photography ● real estate ● inspections.
Buying or leasing a drone..?	1 Most hobbyists, drone racing enthusiasts or recreationist buy their drones: others build their own. Hiring or leasing is for them unlikely unless they are taking a lesson – perhaps with a buy option where the lesson cost is taken back by the buyer of a drone. 2 Commercial drones are offered on terms with include either hire or purchase.
Byelaws	In the UK it is likely that some local authorities and other public and private landowners have used byelaws to formally address possible concerns about the use of drones on their landed estates. Known examples include: **1. Bishopstoke's public open spaces** Drones are included in byelaws is Bishopstoke Parish Council. The council's public open spaces, walks etc are covered the words in the table.

(Byelaws continued)

Extract from the byelaws of Bishopstoke Parish Council

Quote:
"....PART 5 - MODEL AIRCRAFT, DRONES AND OTHER AIRBORNE DEVICES
General prohibition

24. No person shall cause any power-driven model aircraft, drones or other airborne devices to:

(a) take off or otherwise be released for flight or control the flight of such an aircraft or drone from the ground; or
(b) land on the ground without reasonable excuse. ..."

It may be noted that the item 24(b) seems to allow for the landing a drone in say, an emergency.

2. **Military establishments**
   The Ministry of Defence byelaws for bases and other establishments were reviewed in 2013-2014. It seems that drones were included as a measure against unauthorised photography.
3. **National Trust**
   National Trust policy is reflected in the organisation's byelaws.
   See page 65 **National Trust policy.**
4. **Sandringham Estate**
   The several thousands of hectares of Her Majesty's home estate are protected by a prohibition on over-flying with drones unless prior permission has been given. It is not clear whether a geofence has been installed against unauthorised intrusion.

C

cameraship	A drone fitted with a camera used exclusively for photography or other imagery. A light-weight camera allows longer flight times.
Camera Surveillance – Certification	In the UK, anybody carrying out public service or commercial drone surveillance operations with cameras is required to comply with the surveillance camera code of practice of the Surveillance Commissioner and be able to demonstrate so doing. Certification follows the successful completion of two steps: 1. Desk top study 2. Visit and audit by the Surveillance Commissioners authorised and accredited auditors.
Cargo drones system	The transportation of cargo in a region will need an infrastructure and organisation. It will probably include the following components: • air corridors with a width of 200 metres and height of 150 metres • geo-fencing of inter-hub routes • hubs in selected locations for refuelling batteries etc, hangers for storing cargo, garaging ground equipment • covered areas with equipment for unloading and re-batching loads.
Caves, tunnels and underground voids	Bradford University is developing a drone to explore tunnels under the city. Applications of underground work are conceivable in a) speleology - for cave exploration and emergency incidents, b) sewers and drains – for inspections, and d) voids underground – for roof falls in mines and caves.
Certificate of Waiver or Authorisation	When a commercial drone user applied for and obtained an exemption of an operation eg. under section 333, a Certificate of Waiver or Authorisation was issued with it by the FAA. The COA allows the operation subject to any conditions. (Now not available - from 23 June 2016).
charger	Device which recharges a spent or partly spent battery.
Charging of a battery (1)	Recreational drones fly for about 20 minutes before a recharging of the battery is required. Most hobbyists carry several batteries in a specially designed bag, eg LiPo bag. Where a drone is on standby for say, deliveries, one approach for a prospective coffee delivery service is to have a stack of drone-shelves with each having a charging point for a drone.
Charging of a battery (2)	Some drones are solar powered, eg Zephyr, so batteries which are carried could be recharged from the sun's energy.

CIA (Confidentiality, Integrity, and Availability)

A cybersecurity term which concerns the confidentiality, integrity, and availability of data. It is used to denote clusters of relevant characteristics of data in internet systems or in IoT devices which might be threatened during a cyber-attack on any of their vulnerabilities.

For instance, the spoofing of a UAV is a form of cyberattack on the operating systems of the device whereby the drone's data is no longer:

- confidential only to the pilot and any other authorised person
- with integrity
- available to the operator and any other authorised person.

circle mode

A set way of flying where the drone flies continuously in a circle of predetermined radius and altitude, with the nose pointing to the centre. Sometimes referred to as *orbit me* or *point of interest*.

Cloud

In this book the term cloud is used in three ways:

1. the ordinary meaning of a mass of water vapour in the sky
2. the digital data storage "common"
3. the cluster of imagery points used in certain types of 3D and other photogrammetry techniques.

Coal industry

India Coal will probably be using drones for:

- assessing landscapes for restoring mining areas with green works
- assessing land for the extraction of coal
- assessing coal stock yards to determine stocks and depletion and renewal rates.

Coastguard – Antarctica sea ice surveillance

Resupply icebreaker ships travelling to McMurdo Station have used drones to spot routes in difficult sea ice conditions. Drones replaced aircraft to avoid risk to personnel.
A Puma AE drone was used, having the following features: a) flight duration of 3.5 hours, b) range of nearly 10 miles, and c) weight of 13.5 pounds.

Codes for drones

As the use of drones has developed and grown codification of usage for particular purposes has been a concurrent development. This item merely identifies known codes and reflects on their rationale.
Although some codes have originated under statute, others are from professional bodies and other non-government organisations. Generally, when working, professional and or voluntary codes of good or best practice should be observed unless the professional ones are mandatory then they must be observed – essentially as a minimum standard. Statutory codes must be observed unless better practice can be proved to be better practice.

Code		Oversight - Code - Comment
Disaster aid	International (Voluntary - advisory)	• International aid agencies and their associated emergency services • Model regulations, rules or code - yet to be adopted • For areas of natural and other disasters
Flying	UK (Statutory)	• Civil Aviation Authority • The Drone Code
Journalism	USA (Professional practice)	• Professional Society of Drone Journalists • Code of ethics for Drone Journalists
Journalism	Australia (Academic practice - advisory)	• University of Adelaide has prepared guidance on drone work • a code of best practice with animals

Table: Codes for drones

See page 91 **Wild animals**

Collision avoidance methods

Relatively heavy drones have the technology to be able to sense and avoid other drones, obstructions and aircraft by the following:

- radar
- line of sight flying.

A vulnerability of small drones is they are incapable of taking on radar equipment. However, some may be fitted with equipment enabling appropriate responses to geofencing technology.

Combat drones

Combat UVAs are deployed in theatres of conflict by many military forces of sovereign states and other groups for various purposes or missions, including:

- battlefield high level persistence surveillance • border patrols
- casualty extraction (in development) • combat action or strikes
- decoys in aerial combat • delivery of supplies

Combat drones continued

- improvised explosive device (IED) searches for convoys
- intelligence, surveillance and reconnaissance (ISR)
- jamming other aircraft, drones, etc • kamikaze or suicide drone attacks
- general and satellite-like surveillance • theatre awareness.

commercial operation

In the UK the ANO 2016 gives commercial operation to mean ..." any operation of an aircraft other than for public transport— (a) which is available to the public; or (b) which, when not made available to the public, is performed under a contract between an operator and a customer, where the latter has no control over the operator, in return for remuneration or other valuable consideration".

Commissioning services and work

When commissioning drone work a client is likely to want prior evidence of the following:

a) the operator's qualifications and CAA permission to fly the drone
b) the mode of work – for instance , that the pilot be accompanied by a colleague to operate equipment, eg a camera
c) insurance cover and current compliance with the terms etc.
d) possibly, a range of previous work in the required type, eg have portfolio
e) general nature of approach to working - procedures protocols and standards - such as: i) risk assessment, ii) flight plan, iii) landowner's permission, etc
f) the quality of the cybersecurity of the UAVS, ie the embedded systems to run the UVA and systems' relating to the on-board sensors
g) terms and conditions of business.

competent observer

The individual who stands beside and assists the person in charge of a UAV when he or she flies it in first person view, eg mainly by spotting hazards. The term is fully defined, for example, in the CAA document of 28 April 2016, entitled *ANO 2009 ORS4 No 1168 General Exemption E4185 Small unmanned aircraft - First person view (FPV) flying.*

Controlled airspace

Airspace around and between airports within which airliners fly and which is controlled by air traffic controllers in accord with a) international and national standards, b) aircraft flight plans and pilots' requirements.
See page 46 **"inverted wedding cake" poster**
Cf page 89 **Uncontrolled airspace**

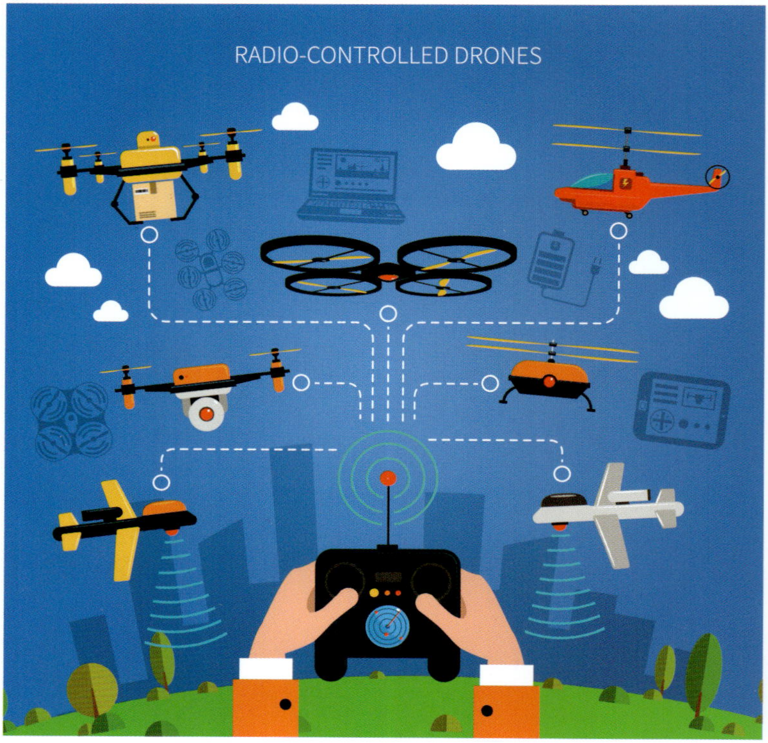

Controller/flight controller

The handheld device or desk-based unit for wireless or sometimes satellite communication by which the pilot transmits and receives messages for flying the UAV. (It is known colloquially as "transmitter".)
See page 11 **autonomous flying**
See page 39 **ground control station**

Cooperative research and development agreement (CRDA)

A form of contact under statute between a USA government agency and a private sector company or university to undertake research and development into a technological topic so as to advance the market for the subject matter.

Countermeasures against drones

A number of systems have been developed, trialled and adopted by the military, aviation industry and others to counter intrusive drones. For instance, the FAA's Pathfinder Program includes an evaluation of at least three kinds of countermeasure for drones – those developed by Gryphon, Liteye and Sensofusion.
The table gives countermeasures to hunt and capture or destroy a drone.

Countermeasures against drones

Countermeasure	Comment
Blighter Anti-UAV Defence System	1. Blighter AUDS – a defence system which uses several technological systems against an intruding UVA so as to a) scan and detect, b) track, c) classify and d) disturb the controller's connection and camera.
Blighter A400 Series	UK's Blighter Surveillance Systems offer several detection systems with different characteristics, such as the drone's speed, distance from the protected asset, direction of approach, etc.
Drone air-to-air net	A drone with FPV to combat intrusive drones has been developed in the USA for air-to-air capture. The FPV pilot's drone has a net and chases the intruding drone. When within range, the FPV-pilot fires the net towards the intruder drone – the latter is enveloped and falls or is carried to the ground.
DroneShield	Using acoustic detection and a database systems technology. DroneShield will recognise the type of intruding drone and create alerts to clients of shielded assets.
Eagles and Falcons	In the Netherlands 100 police officers are using eagles trained to bring down drones which may be flown for criminal purposes. Similarly, Danish police are trialling the use of falcons. UK's Metropolitan Police are reviewing the use of raptors.
Skytracker	Early in 2016 the FAA tested CACI's Skytracker - an anti-drone system for detecting intrusive drones at commercial airports and other locations. It can 'spot' a drone and detect the operator's location. A perimeter line of sensors surround the airport and in effect create a geofence. Once it detects the intruding drone's radio frequencies it triangulates the two locations.
Skywall	A bazooka-like device produced by Open Works Engineering fires a net to capture an intruding drone, bringing it down to earth by parachute.

The film Top Gun 2 covers drone warfare and military drone counter-measures.

Crash reporting

Much will depends on the severity of the incident. The "ins and outs" may be complex and a party may need advice!
USA In essence, a crash must be reported to a) the National Transportation Safety Board, b) FAA, c) the insurer and d) perhaps, the party's attorney.
UK In essence, a crash must be reported to a) the Air Accident Investigation Board (AAIB), b) CAA, c) the police and d) the party's insurer.

Crowd control

1. **Civilian use of riot control agents** There are several examples of drones capable of carrying riot control agents (RCA), such as tear gas and other non-lethal calmatives and incapacitants for crowd control.

2. **War use of riot control agents** It seems that although permitted under international law for civilian use, RCAs are not allowed in warfare.

Crowd funding

"Crowd funding" is now a common way of raising business funds for a UVAS project.

The initiator appeals to the public at large to donate a relatively small sum towards the cost of the project. Such appeals are online and the genuine ones are dealt with by specialist intermediaries with the issue of appropriate documentation on the mission, programme, SWOT analysis (possibly), and anticipated outcomes.

Cybersecurity

One or more drones have been tested at John Hopkins University for vulnerabilities to a cyber-attack. The researchers found several ways of interfering with the UAVs and at least one manufacturer has received a Vulnerability Disclosure Package (VDP) about their drone.

Five cybersecurity breach approaches were used. One was like a DDoS a drone was overwhelmed with 1000 messages.

As with many current Internet of Things (IoT) products the concerns may need to be addressed, for example by a) consumers in commercial and recreational drone markets needing some personal development in cybersecurity, information services, insurance packages, b) the drone industry needing to formulate standards and devise cybersecurity measures to meet possible hacking, and c) manufacturers and suppliers may wish to develop their vulnerability disclosure policy in prospect of receiving a VDP.

Data, Development and Demonstration flights insurance

D

Cover is for flights which are neither for sport or recreation, nor for payment as business or work. The insurance is offered by the BLMA to members who need it as an extension to their sports and recreation drones insurance. It indemnifies or protects individual member for unremunerated flights when they are collecting data, demonstrating or testing new products or learning See page 68 of *RC Flight Camera Action*, March 2016.

See page 43 **Insurance law for drones**

Data protection

Unless exempt, an organisation operating a drone in the UK and recording and processing personal information, eg photographs, must register under the *Data Protection Act 1998* with the Office of the Information Commissioner. (See https://ico.org.uk/)
The personal data must be kept in accord with the data protection.

Data protection principles

Drone users who collect personal information are required to have regard to the eight data protection principles given in *Schedule 1* of the *Data Protection Act 1998.*

daylight operations

"Daylight-only operations" are defined as being from the official sunrise to the official sunset at the local time. In practice terms this is half hour before sunrise to half hour after sunset.

Defibrillator by drone

A drone which is built as a flying automated external defibrillator (AED) is used in a town in the Netherlands. When a person suffers cardiac arrest it sent and monitored by doctors who supervise the lay person administering treatment. It can be delivered within about one minute over an area of 4.6 square miles.
Similarly, in New Zealand an inventor has designed a defibrillator-carrying drone.

An early delivery after the incident is of the essence since a delivery time of more than say eight to 10 minutes means almost zero chances of survival with no brain impairment. The earlier the application of an AED is made, the better the chances of surviving the death. (Of course, the application of cardiopulmonary resuscitation (CPR) will prolong survival chances without brain damage.)

Delivery drones

Delivery of cargo by drone for either civilian or military purposes is or is being developed by several organisations. Examples include:

- Defibrillators (See page 22 **Defibrillator by Drone**)
- Goods – Amazon are trialling drones for delivery of goods
- Medicines, drugs and clinical equipment (See page 40 **Health and Care Deliveries**)
- Military supplies – the US Marines and the US Army have used or are trialling the deployment of drones to deliver supplies in battle zones
- Organ transplant donations – trialling of system is underway in India and the USA. See page 67 **Organ donation transport**.

Delivery services

Delivery services by drone exist or are being developed.

Delivery services

Country	Service and comments
Germany	DHL have a cargo delivery service to islands in the North Sea and in mainland Germany. See page 68 **Packstation**.
Kenya	Astral Aviation have announced development towards offering a small cargo drone delivery service in Kenya – and beyond if the current drafting of regulations would allow
South Korea	The government is trialling drones for home deliveries in two stages: (i) drones lifting and carrying packages of up to 5kg – to 2018, and (ii) drones carrying packages to homes – to 2020.
Rwanda	A medical delivery drone service run by USA Ziplines and other companies to about 20 clinics is to operate in the country. It will be by automated flying with a range of 120km and a payload of about 1.5kg

table continued from previous page

Country	Service and comments
UK and USA	Amazon is trialling a delivery services in the UK and USA. The service may start elsewhere. The company have different drones for different environments. A trial home delivery by an autonomously flown drone in an urban setting has been achieved in Nevada. Safe conditions were observed by (i) a standby pilot and several observers en route, (ii) a vacant house was used for the delivery, and (iii) the neighbourhood was quiet.

Developing a service

It might be borne in mind that there are many areas of work involved in developing a drone strategy for a drone business at national and local service levels:

- ensure and show proof of concept
- procure funding for expenditure on capital items and initial consumables
- obtain CAA's Airworthiness Approval Note AAN for the drones – covering scope and modifications
- write flight plans and safety plans
- obtain the range of insurances for commercial operations with UAVs
- seek partners or stakeholders, as appropriate, to build a strategic plan and its long term improvement of procedures, eg procurement, education and training
- devise the functional specification for the drone, and procuring and adapting a suitable model
- comply with Civil Aviation Authority (CAA) regulations and, if necessary, devising policy for the service with the CAA
- test the drone in realistic scenarios
- ensure data storage
- recruiting, inducting developing and training as needed for pilots, and other role holders in specific cognate scenarios
- training and assessing staff to pilot the drone to a very high standard in typical industrial or emergency situations.

Developments, constructions, buildings and structures

The new drone industry is leading to a few new kinds of development, property and facilities.

Developments, constructions, buildings and structures

Development	Details and comment
Drone enclosure /arena	A facility for flight training • provides an indoor netted enclosure • net covers sides and top • offers drone flying lessons to visitors, racing... • example at Hillier Aviation Museum (USA)
Drone flight schools	A facility for the following: • one or more classrooms for lessons and demonstrations • reception and rest room facilities • secure storage rooms for equipment • shop and display area • indoor or outdoor open space for safe and secure flying lessons and demonstrations. Outdoor space needs to be situated within the Air Navigation Order's requirements.
Drone hub	A place where drone airspace corridors converge and a mix of developments might arise. They may include droneport, health clinic, small scale manufacturing, e-trading and warehouse business, and customs and excise reception
Dronepark	South Korea is reported to have a dronepark comprising: • 2.7ha in Seoul • Information centre • Limitations are 30 users who have pre-booked • Flying UAV under 12kg under 150m
Droneport	Based on work by Lord Foster, a cargo facility located in place for: • the landing and reception of cargo carrying drones • unloading, re-batching and reloading of cargo • the launching of empty or cargo carrying drones • repair and routine maintenance of UAVSs • associated other developments, eg post and courier

table continued from previous

Developments, constructions, buildings and structures	
Development	**Details and comment**
Military Ground control station Bunker - need not be on the same site	1. Ground control station - Temporary or permanent accommodation cockpit or console (office) for the pilot, sensor operator and perhaps intelligence staff for a military drone, eg Predator, comprising: • two tables – workstations - each fitted with a monitor, computer key board bracketed by a throttle and joystick; beneath were pilot's rudder pedals • wall monitors for real-time aerial depictions of surveillance and other imager • workstation for the intelligence staff. 2. bunker and hanger – accommodation for: • protective shielding for UAVS when on ground • hanger for shelter from hostile action or severe weather • repair and maintenance facilities • crew accommodation and rest and recreation facilities
Packstation and compound	DHL's Parcelcopter Skyport is example, being an unmanned shed-like container with fully automated equipment for the following operations: • takes a customer's parcel through a key-pad opening • deposits the parcel in a container • the container fitted, as part of the fuselage, into a delivery drone (Parcelcopter) which is on the roof of the "shed". • Parcelcopter takes off towards destination • On arrival the automated process is a the same in reverse order • At the end of the last delivery, when the drone is not in use, nor being maintained, it is effectively housed in an automated roof-top hanger; the unit's roof panels close together to form a secure enclosure/garage. The drone delivers the parcel to another packstation where the recipient collects it by

table continued from previous

Packstation and compound	dialling in a code on the keypad fixed near the closed door of the deposit box. All of the operations are automated, even the closing of the roof panels to create the secure hanger
Drone race courses (informal)	a. Many drone race courses are informally set up by enthusiasts in a farmer's fields in places re mote from buildings and structures. b. Similarly, indoor race courses are set up informally by enthusiasts in otherwise disused covered carparks, warehouses, and other buildings. c. The European Rotor Sports Association used Wembley Stadium to hold drone racing event. The event featured provided banked turns, barrel rolls, a players' tunnel and slaloms.
Drone racing league	As yet drone league racing is embryonic and no permanent race establishments are known in the UK.
Drone service station	Airbase of Israel is an example of a service station for a commercial drone where a returning drone is housed and the battery changed by an automated system. One might expect an automated digital pre-flight check is part of the service, etc
Drone test sites	In the UK and the USA several test sites have been initiated to carry out research, trials and the like in to aspects of practical concerns about UAV aviation.

Directed energy weapons (DEW)

The table shows examples of directed energy weapons.

Directed energy weapons (DEW)

Technology	Comments
Laser	• may be used to destroy a flying drone • sometimes used for temporarily blinding • as a weapon on a drone
Light	• sometimes used for temporarily blinding
Sound	• long range acoustic devices (LRAD) to give messages, warnings and pain
Wireless	• drones may be used for jamming, decoy purposes

Disasters and drones

The use of drones after a disaster will depend on several matters, namely:

1. the nature and characteristics of the particular disaster
2. the resilience planning of the local government and public emergency bodies, etc
3. the awareness, information and preparedness of local residents and businesses etc
4. the level and continuity of the wireless connectivity systems remaining after the event. Some kinds of disaster may/will obliterate or knock-out connectivity temporarily. Without connectivity several drone mounted services based on the Internet of Things would not be available to the operating emergency and rescue teams.

In the UK drones may be used in any scheme of Community Resilience Planning which is (possibly) intended to cover every eventuality for a) emergency and rescue, b) sustaining life post-event, c) aftermath clear-up, etc.

With connectivity etc, drones could be used as follows:

a) to seek persons trapped in a buildings, eg using body heat detection equipment
b) to photograph damaged buildings and structures
c) to attach sensors to unstable buildings
d) to explore voids and insides of places - to set priorities for making-safe, clearance, etc
e) to seek displaced and injured persons,

f) to deliver food supplies and emergency or care supplies including AEDs, and

g) to drop lifebuoys to aid those in the sea or other waters.

See page 16 **Codes for drones**
See page 38 **Global code of conduct for drones**

disruption

A major change in the way an organisation, business, industry or profession, etc goes about its business or some aspect of it. Drones are causing such changes to work practices, eg battlefield practice.

Disruptive drone /drone technologies

Descriptive of a drones as such and/or technology used with drones as a system which change the way, for instance, an industry, profession, or military service goes about business or some aspect of business.

"Drone"

1. **General meanings** The book hones in on the subject of unmanned aerial vehicles, aka drones. However, the word has meanings more commonly associated with other things, such as: a) a male bee, b) a low monotonous humming sound, eg as from a bagpipe's drone aka drone pipe, c) a person who is idle, d) a speaker who talks at length, and often associated with the listener's boredom!

2. **General aviation meanings** An interpretation of the term drone needs to be made in the context in which it is used by the speaker or writer. Generally, and in this book, it is usually regarded as a colloquial term referring to any device being:

- an unmanned aerial vehicle (UAV)
- an unmanned aerial vehicle system (UAVS) where one or more human beings are involved in remotely launching, flying and landing it on a purposeful mission involving the payload.

Drones are available in three basic flying forms of different sizes, weights, functions, and use classifications. The three basic forms are: 1) single rotor drone, 2) multicoptor – which are usually a tricoptor, quadcoptors or a hexacoptor, and 3) fixed wing drone.

See page 6 **Aircraft - meaning applied to drones**
See page 90 **Weight**

3. **Ground and sea meanings** However, the term drone is also used to mean *unmanned ground vehicles* (UGVs), or marine floating vehicles and/or submersibles. Also, at least one drone is capable of flying, floating and submersing.

Dronecode	The CAA's set of requirements or rules for flying a drone in the UK - they provide what the pilot of a drone must observe and are set out in various documents - see Part 1.
Drone Information Notice (DIN)	A notice available to drone users which gives details of a facility where a new or changed No Drone Zone has been issued.
drone journalism code	A non-statutory code of conduct as to how journalists should behave when reporting on drones and drone-related matter and /or using drones in the course of their work.
Droneport or skyport	1. Generally a place where drone corridors converge, being a facility located in place for the reception, unloading, re-batching and reloading of cargo which is brought and taken away on an unmanned aerial vehicle system. 2. The FAA is currently working on regulations for droneports as a result of a local decision to create one on 50 acres at Eldorado Valley. See page 68 **Packstation**
Drone strategy in UK	Workshops conducted from December 2015 to February 2016 by the Department for Transport, the Ministry of Defence and Sciencewise will be used to formulate the government's drone strategy of the UK. It will be published later in 2016.
Eagles	See page 20 **Table: Counter measures against drones**
Earthquake relief	Drones have been used after several earthquakes • **Ecuador** - small solar-powered drones were used to photograph damaged areas. • **Nepal** - a fund raising effort was mounted for earthquake aid by Paul Borrud using photographs on dronation.com. See page 38 **Global code of conduct for drones**
Education and training 1	Aspects of education and training are shown in the table. There are some courses at universities, colleges and drone training establishments which include cognate aspects droneology in their syllabuses. Examples are shown in the table.

Education and training	
Aspect	**Comment**
University of Adelaide	• has devised a guide to good practice when working with animals • seeking to offer accredited training to students and others
Flight training schools	• offer lessons in flying to hobbyists • more rigorously, the BNUC and BNUC-S and other professional level programmes for prospective commercial pilots See page 12 **BNUC and BNUC-S**
Simdrone	• training simulator which offers real time simulations of flying fixed wing and helicopter drones. • number of simulation scenarios in different kinds of environment –urban, rural and wild.
Southampton University	• offers a master's degree course • covers design and building of a drone (UVA) focused for particular functions

Educating and training 2

On 4 May 2016 the FAA issued a Memorandum entitled *Educational use of unmanned aerial systems* which gives its interpretation of the law on the use of drones by students on aviation-related courses in educational establishments. It also mentions faculty staff involvement and as a separate pointer drones for hobbies and recreation.

Electricity distribution grids

The inspection for maintenance and repair of electricity grids cover extensive lineal distances. The work would involve considerable staff travel. Drones offer a means of low-cost, low-resource inspection of relatively quickly.

The range of activities which may be included are: a) land mapping and 3D scanning for optional future gridlines, b) routine inspections of towers and cable lines, and c) identifying storm damage, including fallen trees and forest road and other route blockages.

In the USA an inspection service company is able to detect electrical installations and has worked drones in eight states covering over 300,000 miles of cables and towers, 1,000 transformer stations and gas stations and at least a dozen large generating stations.

electro-adhesion	A technology whereby a nano-drone on landing adheres to the surface, eg a vertical wall, by electrostatic force.
Emergency services training	In the UK the emergency services – ambulance, including HARTs; fire and rescue; and police - are increasingly using drones in synergetic ways at fires and other emergency scenes. At least one UAVS training company – Sky Futures - which had offered each service a separate course, now provides integrated courses to jointly meet the needs of the various services.
Energy industry	The energy industry is employing in-house or professional drone service companies to address everyday tasks and emergencies. The requirements cover electricity generation and distribution, oil and gas pipeline networks, tidal and wave electricity generation, and wind turbines; they include: • aerial filming and photography of infrastructure assets • emergency response by inspections of damage and destruction, and the delivery of supplies • inspections of assets for damage after earthquakes, landslips, severe snow and other storms • inspections of power lines, oil and gas pipelines and wind turbines • mapping and surveying of land and property assets.
Environments	Many environments have conditions which are normally too extreme for flying drones. Given below are several situations where drones have been flown, perhaps after being adapted: a) asteroids, b) battlefields, d) caves, e) forest and woodland, f) glaciers, g) icebergs and ice seas, h) inside of buildings, i) hail, rain and snow, j) planets, k) snow and ice lands, l) storms and winds, and m) volcanoes.
ESC	Electronic Speed Controller
EU standards for drones	In 2014 the European Commission announced work on proposed standards for RPAS to cover the following: a) aviation safety, b) privacy and data protection, c) security, d) liability and insurance cover, and e) research and development, together with support for the EU drone industry. The implications of Brexit will need to be reviewed with the view that some manufacturers and service providers in the UK will, no doubt, wish to trade within the EU. See page 9 **Airworthiness**
Exclusion zone	Airports, aerodromes, prisons and other critical infrastructure and certain other property almost invariably have exclusion zones imposed on the flying of drones within a specified distance or over them. See page 7 **Airspace - Law**

Exemption under Section 333

Formerly, under section 333 of the Federal Aviation Authority Reform Act 2012, the FAA may, on request, granted regulatory exemption to commercial users subject to conditions.

This was colloquially known as a "section 333 exemption". Some 38 types of business have obtained exemption. The main ones are real estate, inspections, and photography. The availability of new S333 exemptions ended on 21 June 2016 and is replaced by part 107 from 29 August 2016.

The research staff of universities were previously treated as commercial and require exemption unless the university was formally linked with a body already holding section 388 exemption. However, on 4 May 2016 the FAA issued a Memorandum entitled *Educational use of unmanned aerial systems* which a) deals with use of drones by students on aviation-related courses, etc, and b) mentions faculty staff involvement in educational matters.
From 29 August 2016 major changes to the flying rules for certain UVAs are being introduced by the FAA. Otherwise known as part 107.

Explosions

In 2015 assessments of damage to buildings and infrastructure at Tianjin in China were undertaken with drones. The condition of buildings and structures was regarded as hazardous to the investigators making estimates of losses.

Indoor use of drones is not uncommon and care needs to ensure by undertaking a risk assessment that no explosive gases are present in the void where a drone is to be operated.

exposition

A manual or set of official documents which sets out the rules for flying, including or exclusively the administrative and operational requirements for flying an unmanned aerial vehicle (UVA).
New Zealand has a clear and comprehensive – seemingly exemplar - exposition for drone flying, including registration.

"Eyes in the sky"

A colloquial term for the use of drones for land surveying building inspections and the like and perhaps more general surveillance purposes.

Filming over land with drones

Some local authorities and other landowners may allow flying drones in their area subject to the national regulatory regime, any local byelaws, and other requirements: some may not.
See page 13 **Byelaws**
See page 65 **National Trust Policy**

Film production

Drones are used in the making of a films and TV programmes in two ways: 1) aerial shots of scenes, panoramic views etc, 2) as artefacts used in the film itself, for example, founder of the *Drone Ops*, Justin Pringle, had made several designs of drones for films, such as *Star Wars*.

Firefighting

F

Firefighting in complex buildings, structures and inaccessible wild lands growth lends itself to drone-based approaches which enable increased speed of action, savings of resources and other advantages.
See page 32 **Emergency services training**
Some DJI drones receive wildfire alerts for on-board geofencing
See page 91 **Wildfires**

***Fireproof Aerial Robot System* (FAROS)**

A firefighting drone being developed in South Korea having the following equipment:

- an altimeter – to measure height
- image-processing technology – to locate where the fire began
- an inertia measurement unit sensor – to assist navigation
- a thermoelectric cooling system
- a thermal-imaging camera - to recognize objects or people inside a building
- a 2D-LiDAR sensor.

Qualities of FAROS are that it is fireproof to 1,000 C and flame-retardant.

---

first person view (FPV)

Piloting a UAV by means of a front-mounted camera on the drone and though goggles worn by the pilot or some other device. Here the pilot is generally unaware of the wider scene or environment and is required to have an observer using natural sight (maybe corrected) but without other aids.

The rule about line-of-sight at 500 metres applies to FPV, but the observer rather than the pilot is required to maintain visual contact.
The regulations pertaining to FPV include CAA document of 28 April 2016 entitled *ANO 2009, ORS4 No 1168, General Exemption E4185 Small unmanned aircraft - First person view (FPV) flying.*
See page 102 **British FPV Racing Association (League)**
See page 18 ***Competent observer***
See page 62 **Modes**

Piloting a UAV

Fish and fishing

Drones are used in the fishing sector in several ways:

- enforcement of fishing law
- fishing, eg baited fishing lines being carried beyond normal reach
- shark protection and protecting swimmers from sharks.

See page 58 **Marine Nature Reserves**

flight clearance

Briefly, the status or process of either a) obtaining permission to fly a UAV in civilian and/or military controlled airspace, or b) permission to use a drone for one or more routine operations.

flight controller

See page 19 **controller**

Flight planning

At the moment flight planning is particularly important for commercial and military pilots: most recreationists and hobbyists probably use less formal approaches unless complying with competition rules which require a specified form of plan.

Flight planning may be described in at least two ways as follows:

1. Planning a flight using waypoints so as to fly a route autonomously – there are many software programs for flight planning (perhaps with telemetry and post-flight analytics).

Flight planning continued

2. Possibly, the planning of the whole or parts of the procedure for a flight including: a) pre-fight checks, both UAVs's and weather, b) route plan, eg using way points, c) setting telemetry requirements for the flight (but this may be automatic), d) adoption of standardised operational procedures (as related to the commercial or military mission), and e) adopting a readiness of the requirements for any emergency response plan (ERP), and f) adoption of settings for post flight analysis of telemetry.

Flooding and drones

Drones have been used in England and Scotland where flooding occurred or was expected. Purposes to which they were put included: a) evaluating the likelihood of flooding in an area, b) identifying property likely to be affected by flood waters, and c) assessing the damage caused by flood water to buildings.

Flying a drone and connectivity

There are several modes of flying a drone, all of which depend on wireless connectivity, namely: a) autonomous flight, eg DHL's delivery drones to islands in the North Sea, b) *first person view* (FPV) flying, c) *line-of-sight* (LOS) flying - generally required for flying recreational drones, and d) *remote flying* - as in remote split operations.

Forestry operations

The uses of drones for forestry operations include: a) mapping, b) assessments of topography for roads and drainage patterns, c) measuring tree heights, and d) measuring canopy densities.

In India one administration is considering drones although trials have been inconclusive. Poaching of elephants, insurgents and smuggling of timber are the main concerns. However, during trials the heavy canopy blocked the view.

In Switzerland algorithms have been developed from 20,000 photographs to enable drones with an artificial intelligence capability to track paths in forests and mountains.

frame 1

The body or hull of a drone without any operational components, such as micro-computers, motors, propellers, receiver, transmitter, undercarriage and the like.

frame 2

As in a film which is made up of images in 'frames'.
A measure here is 'fpm' or frames per minute.

Franchise and drones

It seems that most franchises are based on a specified named business service or product. In the case of UAVs the named drone business could be modelled in this way and may well be. However, another franchise model is to develop a mix of services and products to set up a drone business in any one of the business sectors – in other words the franchise is about setting up a drone business.

Fuel

Drones are usually powered by lithium polymer batteries, eg most recreational drones. Other fuels include a) chemically-based fuel cells (Stalker XE240 drone), b) hydrogen fuel cell, c) ground based laser for refuelling, d) solar power (Zephyr). See page 37 **Power driven**
Power sources

Gas pipelines

As a trial the Gas Authority of India (GAIL) monitors 200km of gas pipeline against a) erosion of soil, b) exposure to weather, c) sabotage, d) unauthorised building works, and e) unauthorised excavations.

geofence

G

A geofence is a virtual barrier around an area of land, eg a nuclear power station or a ship, which warns the owner or occupier of a possible intrusion by a UAV. The drone user may also be warned of the geofence.

Moves are being made in the USA to formulate a regulatory regime to control intrusive drones. On aspect is for the installation of geofences around sensitive buildings, estates and infrastructures.

UVAs are available with installed devices carrying geofencing software. The software carries data on exclusions zones and is capable of being updated in real time.

The system has the following characteristics: a) flying the drone avoids exclusion zones, b) the software can be overridden except when the exclusion zone is of national security importance, and c) if the user has verified status, the operator may override the software subject to conditions.
See page 17 **collision avoidance methods**

Geological field work

Drones are used extensively in geological work, such as: a) exploration and mapping potential areas of mineral deposits in remote areas, b) inspection of pipelines and other infrastructure equipment, and c) assessing volumes of heaped extracted minerals.

gimbal

A mounting on a drone for an item of equipment, eg a camera, which keeps the item level and steady when the drone is flying or hovering, eg in windy conditions.

A gimbal has either two or three axes, and they are described as "2 axis" and "3 axis" respectively – the latter correcting rotation movements on roll, pitch and yaw.

Glaciers and drone mapping

Several studies of glaciers have used drones for mapping and other work, such as: a) glacier surfaces with 3D DEM mapping (Fox Glacier – University of Canterbury, New Zealand, b) Outburst floods from glaciers have been mapped by Sfm photogrammetry (Greenland – University of Leeds).

In 2014 a drone was used to measure glacier depletion by taking numerous photographs and creating a 3D map from a height of 100metres. The map was compared with that for aerial photographs in 2003. Then interpretation from a photogrammetry study gave details ice area changes and loss of the ice.

See page 65 **Navigation control connectivity**

global code of conduct for drones

A proposed agreement by international aid agencies which provides a best practice statement or set of rules for using drones in areas of natural or man-made disaster.

global positioning system (GPS)

A satellite-based information and communication technology (ICT) by which military, commercial and recreational drones may be navigated autonomously in real-time.

GPS aerial

Antenna-like component to receive and transmit satellite locational or map referenced communications.

See page 89 ***Waypoint***

Grants for Agriculture and Horticulture

In the UK government grants to support the use of drone to enhance agricultural and horticultural productivity are available.
There are conditions, including:

- up to 40% of specified costs are given
- applications may be made for as much as £2,500 but not more than £35,000

Specified costs include:
- a drone (UAV) or drone-like vehicle, eg a tractor
- a sensor mountable on the drone, etc
- crop management software for data collection and analysis

The purpose of the project needs to be one or more of the following:

- areas of crop green leaf - monitoring
- disease - detection
- fertiliser requirements - evaluation
- water stress - detection
- weed - detection
- yields of crop – estimations and monitoring.

Gremlins Project

A DARPA programme to devise and evaluate a swarm drone concept for multi-various purposes in combat theatres, particularly electronic attacks on enemy battlefield systems. Possible missions of gremlins – in thousands, rather than dozens of units - include:

- decoys
- intelligence, reconnaissance, surveillance
- jamming of enemy aircraft and battlefield electronic systems
- kamikaze.

It is likely the relatively inexpensive gremlins would be a) launched in the battle zone by air-to-air deployment from large aircraft, b) carryout missions in networked arrays, c) recovered by the mothership for maintenance and refuelling, and d) relaunched for further missions up to say 20 times.

ground control station (GCS)

A ground-based cockpit or console (office) for the pilot and sensor operator of a military drone, eg Predator, generally comprising two tables, work-stations, each fitted with a monitor, computer key board bracketed by a throttle and joystick; beneath were pilot's rudder pedals.
Once a drone is made airborne by a separate launch and landing line-of-sight team (usually far away from the GCS), the pilot remotely flies the UAV using the control apparatus. The sensor operator's apparatus are used to control the targeting pod of the drone.

The personnel in the GCS for the P1HH Hammerhead, a medium altitude long range (MALE) drone, can simultaneously manage two operational UAVSs and one in transit.

Ground penetrating radar (GPR)

Trials with a drone carrying ground penetrating radar (GPR) are being conducted. If successful they will enable farmers and others, eg archaeologists, working in former combat zones to detect landmines.

Guidelines

The USA-based Remote Control Ariel Platform Association (RCAPA) publishes a set of comprehensive guidelines in several categories, such as a) general, b) building and aircraft tests, maintenance/log books.

gyroscope /gyro

A sensor which detects rotational movement around three dimensional straight line directions. (Invented by Elmer Sperry (1911).
Cf See page 5 **accelerometer**

Hacking

H

Claims of hacking into drones have been made, so cybersecurity concerns may need to be addressed by manufacturers, and user organisations involved with drones. Issues may include:

- inadequate penetration testing against hacking of cyber vulnerabilities
- release of UAVSs by manufacturers with potential vulnerabilities for cyber attack
- unauthorised use or collection of data which has be accumulated by a business for its own use or on behalf of a client
- unauthorised take-over by hackers and using cyber control of a drone and its use for criminal or terrorist purposes
- hacking attacks on military drones.

Hazards

Hazards which may hamper prevent or interfere with flying or other drone operations include:

- aircraft
- balloons – free, moored or tethered
- drone counter-measures
- efflux from chimneys
- fireworks and pyrotechnic displays
- geofences
- gliders, kites, microlights, paragliders, parachutes
- jamming
- light, laser, etc from search lights and other devices
- model aircraft including other UAVs
- rockets and other projectiles
- smoke from fires in the open, whether controlled or wild
- spoofing
- structures, eg buildings, cranes, steeples and towers
- weapons firing shells and other projectiles.

Hazard mapping

Drones are used in the Philippines to map potential environmental hazards, eg landslides, tsunamis and the like.

Health and care deliveries

In Africa at least six countries are using drones on health programmes to deliver medical supplies to health workers in remote rural areas, and areas cut-off by floods, etc. In one example it was stated that a two day journey by road vehicle takes about 30 minutes by drone.

Hire of pilots

Many drone companies offer services for hire in one or more business sectors. Pilots are qualified with the CAA's FCAW and hold insurance for types of commercial drone work.
See page 103 **Drone Safe Register**

Health and care deliveries

Hive	Collective term for a swarm of drones which are launched singly or together and flown in a coordinated manner.
Hobbyist drones	See page 103 **Drone Safe Register** See page 84 **Sport and recreation drones**
Hobby grade	A drone which is suitable for recreational use rather than a commercial business use.
Home deliveries	See page 23 **Delivery services**

ID number

Under national registration systems for drones, an ID number is a unique identifying term of letters and numerals which is held for each of the owner's UAVs, or possibly just the owner. The UAV is usually marked.
See page 76 **Registration**

Indoor flying and in enclosed spaces

I

It is not uncommon for drones to be used, eg for racing, in enclosed places, such as: a) buildings – rooms, cellars and lofts, b) caves and cave systems, d) hulls of ships, e) possibly, pipelines, f) silos and other fabricated tanks, g) tunnels and culverts, and h) volcanoes.

Each void is a different context is likely to have different flying and adaptations for risk-avoidance requirements. These are essentially:

- confirmation of adequate and appropriate insurance cover
- the size of the drone is important
- space and ceiling height
- measures for the protection of fabrics and chattels to prevent damage from down draught
- use of an indoor hull
- as far is known, no UAV is explosion-proof so flying inside a building or void should be risk-assessed in the possible event of explosive gases, vapours or substances being present.

In the UK the CAA regulatory regime for outdoors flying is not applicable indoors.
See page 73 **propeller guard**

Indoor hull

An 'indoor hull' is a singular or foursome circular safety guard or fitting for a drone's rotary blades, particularly for quadcopters. They are recommended for flying indoors where the possibility of hitting a family spectator or obstructive furniture or fittings is greater than outside. When fitted they are likely to mean less damage to the blades.

Infrared library

Stored data of infrared images built up to support future ISR operations, whereby a UAVS on an ISR mission autonomously "sees" or fortuitously picks up an image of something on the ground and transmits it to the library for identification.

Inheritance tax liability

For UK death duties, where the deceased owned a drone at the time of death its value on the date of death is added to the gross value of the estate for the purpose of calculating any inheritance tax due to the HMRC.
See page 91 **Will**

Insurance – drone rentals

At least one reinsurance company is offering drones to rent so that the client insurer companies may carry out inspections of damaged properties following a flood or explosion. It may be expected that the estimates of damage may be improved. The package includes: a) regulatory compliance, b) qualified operators, c) drones carrying photographic apparatus, d) output of imagery, and e) relevant data of damage.

Insurance law for drones

The BMFA has identified insurance for drones as a being in three groupings:

1. Sport and recreation insurance – which they provide for their members insurance
2. Commercial work insurance – which is available from commercial and other market sources for commercial drone businesses
3. Data, Development and Demonstration Flights insurance – which is available from the BMFA as an extension to members who need it
   See *RC Flight Camera Action, March, 2016, page 68*

The law requires the pilot flying a commercial drone of less than 500kg weight to have a minimum of 0.75 Million SDR's (Special Drawing Rights) third party liability insurance. This includes war, terrorism and sabotage coverage, when flying drones of less than 500kg weight.

The relevant EU law on the requirements for drone insurance is Regulation *(EC) No 785/2004* of 21 April 2004. However, the European Council's objective is to progressively integrate drone law, including that for insurance into the law for airspace as from 2016.

A review of current third-party insurance in aviation (which mainly applies to manned aircraft) is underway with the view to covering UAVs appropriately as needed.
See page 22 **Data, Development and Demonstration flights insurance**

Insurance industry's concerns

The growth of the commercial and recreational drone market is leading to an increase in underwriting of insurance policies of all kinds. These include drone coverage for insurance policies involving:

- business owner's insurance
- commercial general liability insurance
- farm owner's insurance
- homeowner's insurance
- property owner's insurance.

It seems likely that underwriters will be considering: a) aviation liability, b) directors' and officers' liability, c) drone liability insurance policies, and d) worker's compensation.

Insurance policies

Two main insurance concerns about policies are:

1. policies of insurance for recreational and commercial drone users
2. the adequacy of existing insurance cover already in place for individuals, businesses.

Property owners and others need to check that their existing policies cover damage and injury caused by drones owned by others. It is possible that the policy will have an aviation exclusion.

Commercial insurance cover which might be sought or expected needs to include:

- the requirements demanded by law
- aviation liability
- aviation passenger
- cargo
- data protection and invasion of privacy
- in-flight drone loss or damage
- in-transit for drones and equipment (when on the ground)
- third party cover.

See page 43 **Insurance law for drones**

Insurer's requirements

A drone business seeking insurance cover will need to meet the criteria used by the particular insurance company. In the sense that drone businesses are relatively new the latter is likely to take each application on a one by one basis. The table contains criteria which could be used by an insurance company to evaluate drone-related aspects of a proposed business.

Insurer's requirements

Criterion	Comment
Proof of concept of drone usage	• drones are fit for purpose • manufacturer's involvement in any modifications • fitted into standardised operational procedures
Requirements of the regulatory body	• all aspects of approvals for commercial work were sought and obtained
Pilots	• formal education and training in a) aviation b) drone aviation, • continuing professional development • experience • accident and safety record

table continued from previous

Criterion	Comment
Other staff	• formal education and training in drone maintenance, etc • continuing professional development • experience
Drone modifications, repair and maintenance	• carried out at appropriate times • are always in accord with manufacturer's and regulator's requirements
Drone work and operations	• development of standard operating procedures (SOPs) for drone work • premises and equipment suitable for drone security and for being worked on • equipment is appropriate and maintained • operational protocols, etc are appropriate
Emergency and safety	• handling of emergencies • existence of prepared or adapted emergency response plans (ERPs)
Flights	• flight plans appropriate • operations are at industry standards or better • preflight checks are carried out and action taken as needed • manuals, logbooks and other necessaries are up-to-date and in order • safety record up-to-date and accurate

Intelligence, surveillance and reconnaissance (ISR)

The term ISR denotes a class of military mission for a certain types of military drone with the appropriate technologies when in hostile airspace. See page 61 **Mission – classification of military UAVs**

Internet connectivity

Using a fleet of solar-powered drones, Facebook is reported as intending to increase web internet connectivity to another 4 billion in the world's remoter rural areas. They will fly for 90 days at a time.

Internet of Things (IoT)

A term to denote the way in which devices, eg a drone, and a system, eg its camera, are connected wirelessly together by networks, such as Bluetooth, WiFi, LoRa, satellites, etc, so as to fulfil task or and mission, eg a drone delivery in the North Sea or Africa.

Internet of Things (IoT) and drones

The connectivity concept of IoT is embedded in drones in two broad practical ways

1. flying a drone depends on wireless connectivity, including a) line - of-sight flying, b) first person view (FPV) flying and c) remote flying and d) autonomous flight
2. digital devices mounted on or embedded in a drone will have wireless or satellite connectivity with to transfer data to the operator or to a data store, eg for analytic processing.

"inverted wedding cake" poster

In New Zealand, a poster pictorial representation of controlled airspace, above say, an aerodrome, showing roundels or layers of airspace of different depths and radii.

J

Jamming

For security or defensive purposes, the act of blocking or confusing the GPS signals which the pilot or autonomous system of a drone has generated to navigate the drone. The jammer generates interference in the range of GPS signals used by the pilot.
See page 84 **spoofing**

4K video

A video camera for a drone which is of the highest quality.

K

kamikase

Descriptive of drone designed to be flown at an enemy position with the intention that it explodes there and not return.
Harop (Israel) and *Switchblade* (USA).
See page 61 **Mission - Classification of military UAVSs**
See page 47 **Landing of a drone**

kV rating

The measurement which gives a sense of the strength of a motor in revolutions per minute (Rpm) at a stated voltage when measured at full throttle for a drone without a load.
Rmp = Kv x Voltage

L

Land surveying

Drones lend themselves to land surveying for mapping or other kinds of work. However, the users need to evaluate the type of drone to the type of work and or topography. Generally, land surveyors find they get a good return on capital or short payback period when comparing drone and other capital outlays.

Other benefits arise on safety, in that some situations pose a danger to operators using traditional methods, whereas drones do not require human presence.

Typical work includes:

- calculation of volumes for road construction materials
- creation of high resolution ortho-photographs, topographical surveys and volume models
- generation of point clouds for digital height models
- measurement of difficult to reach objects, such as cave systems, dumps, landfill sites, mining areas and quarries
- photographic and video inspections.

Landing a drone

Landing a drone

Method of Landing	Comment
Arrested	• aircraft carriers are used to land drones by tail hook (on drone) and arrest wire across the deck • a command control station, etc has been installed on USS Carl Vinson for tanker drones – it is assumed this method will be adopted..? Cf page 39 ***ground control station***
Crash	• crash into the ground with a pre-determined break-up of the drone on landing • the break-up is designed to absorb the impact and so prevent or reduce any damage
Electro-adhesion	• which holds a landed drone to say a vertical wall
Hand catch	• catch-in-hand by plucking a hovering or slow-moving drone (may be harmful)
Jamming	• jamming and crashing a drone
Parachute	• rocket-deployed parachute is fitted to the Cormorant drone ambulance for emergency descent • See page 48 ***Netting (2)***
Mid-air Retrieval System (Mars)	• helicopter, catches UVA as it descends by parachute

table continued from previous

Netting (1)	• flying the drone into a ground-based hanging net
Netting (2)	• using a drone to fire a net at intrusive drone and catch it • captured drone parachutes to the ground or is carried to the home base
Raptor catch	• trained raptor eg, eagle, flies to pluck an intrusive drone, so bringing it down to falconer
Remote split operations	• military operation where landing (and taking off) are separate functions from operational flying and sensor work • *Predator* drone is an example
Runway (1)	• horizontal touchdown by remote first-person-view piloting
Runway (2)	• horizontal touchdown by remote line of sight piloting
Spoofing	• spoofing and landing a drone
Transformer	• landing as a UAVS the Black Knight Transformer transforms function • it becomes a truck to carry troops or casualties • may take off as a UAVS but land gain in a safe area to travel further as a truck
Vertical-takeoff and landing (VTOL)	• drone with capability to land in vertical flight after taking off in that way • 'runway independence' is a major merit of VTOL aircraft
Weapon strike	• here a drone is used as a weapon, eg kamikase

Landing a drone (continued)

It may be noted that except in and emergency, the unauthorised landing of a drone may be prohibited or restricted in some way by byelaws, policy statements and other means.

See page 13 **Byelaws**
Cf page 47 **Landing a drone**
See page 65 **National Trust Policy**
See page 78 **Remote split operations**

landing gear

Component of almost all drones which allows a drone to land so as to avoid obstruction or damage to the rotors. There are different forms of landing gear, including:

- collapsible legs to reduce impact damage on crashing
- curved brackets
- electro-adhesive pads, eg for vertical surfaces
- floats for landing on water, but somewhat rare
- protruding legs
- retractable undercarriage wheeled assemblies for larger drones.

Large drones

In the EU large drones, ie those over 150kg, are authorised by the EU aviation regulator but none have been so registered for commercial purposes – all known large drones are at present used by the military serv-ices.

Laser scanning

Drones may be used to create three dimensional mapping, eg by LiDAR in a large number of situations, eg forestry, so providing a cost effective solution, particularly in remote areas.

latency

The period or lag from the moment when a wireless instruction is sent from the controller and the moment when it is given effect in the recipient UAV.

The pilot's capability to deal with latency maybe important when a drone is flown at high speed or confined environments. Possible examples include a) when racing, b) when flying indoors, and c) in combat UAVSs. In racing the latency issue in has been addressed and reduced.
Cf see page 75 ***real time***

lateral axis

The horizontal line from one side to the other side of a drone, that is the port-starboard axis.

Launching a drone

Several ways of launching drones are used according to the situation or type of drone. They are shown in the table

Launching a drone

Type of Launch	Comment
air-to-air launching	• from an aircraft, the eg the swarm drones *Gremlins project* See page 86 **Telescopic drone**
Automated lift-off	• DHL's delivery by drone from a packstation, eg in Germany • *Parceldrone* lifts off autonomously from the roof of the packstation
Catapult	• from a ship or ground location • the drone *ScanEagle* is an example
Ground-to-ground	• a kamikaze or suicide drone • packstation drone (See in this table below *station-to-station)*
Hand launching	• drone is thrown in to the air by the pilot or another (normally within the line of sight of the pilot)
Remote split operations	• common with large military drones, eg *Predator or Reaper* (See page 78)
Station–to-station	• delivery drone such as a parcelcopter and two packstations
Submarine – to-air	• *Blackwing* drone launched from a submarine or unmanned marine vehicle in tube for surveillance or combat
Transformer (UAVS/truck)	• landing as a UAVS the *Black Knight Transformer* transforms function on the ground • it becomes a truck to carry troops or casualties • furthermore it may take off as a UAVS again, but land in a safe area to travel further as a truck

table continued from previous

Type of Launch	Comment
Tube launching Six tube vehicle	• a 3 x six-tube launcher is used as part of a USN low cost unmanned swarming technology project (See page 57 **LOCUST**.) • swarm drones are fired into the air from the ground or a USN ship • uses will be ISR and weapon attacks in a coordinated manner
One tube	• Single tube and air pressure release, eg • Hero-30 (Israel) • Suitable to be portable by an individual
Upward falling payload from seabed	• a DARPA project of seabed pods containing drones • military drones may be kept in a pod on the seabed for long periods
Vertical-takeoff and landing (VTOL)	• most multicopters are VTOL • no known VTOL UAVS military , with mission capability like Predator, has been found • *runway independence* is a major feature of VTOL aircraft and is likely to be increasingly available in the 2020 as a result of current research in the USA and elsewhere

It may be noted that unauthorised launching of a drone may be prohibited or restricted in some way by byelaws, policy statements and other means.

See page 13 **Byelaws**
Cf Page 47 **Landing a drone**
See page 78 **Remote split operations**

Law and drones

Drone law is developed or being developed in many national jurisdictions. It is changing in different ways in numerous countries as the concerns about drones reveal themselves and are sufficiently serious to engage legislators and regulators.

The content of this section is not definitive of the law in any jurisdiction and is intended as an aide memoire on what to consider about the law for those who intend or actually do something.

1. **European Union** In the EU, European aviation law and international aviation law regulates aviation in Europe in three ways, namely
i) general aviation law applies to manned aircraft and to drones
ii) particular aspects of law are applicable only to drones – this aspect of the law is under review at present. (The Brexit decision to leave the EU may affect the outcome..?)
iii) individual member states have developed their own dronelaw.

2. **UK** The CAA has statutory control airspace for drones in the UK. Distinction is made between: a) commercial drones, b) public service, research etc, and c) sports and recreational drones.

3. **USA** The FAA's drone regulations cover the whole country. They distinguish commercial drones and recreational drones. Matters covered include: a) registration, b) approval of drone businesses, c) flying, d) restrictions on flying over or near certain places, and e) airworthiness of drones.

   Although regulations are in place, they have been reviewed and changed by the FAA - so revised rules came into force on 29 August 2016 (see Part 1).
   Pilots may like to note that nearly all states have enacted laws concerning drones but the Federal laws override them in the event of a conflict. Nevertheless state law remains in place until challenged and the matter is determined by the higher court.

See page 76 **Regulatory bodies**
See page 79 **Rules of engagement (ROE) and drones**

Lawyers and drones

In the USA and UK several law firms have developed specialist partners and staff in drone law.

Legislation etc on drones

1. **UK** Legislation on a subject comprises a) statutes (called Acts), and secondary legislation (called statutory instruments) such as regulations and orders). Draft legislation is called a Bill and comes in the form of a draft Act. For instance, for drones the Civil Aviation Act 1965 and the Air Navigation Order 2016 are prime sources of law. Also, the Civil Aviation Authority and other bodies have statutory powers - derived from legislation: a) to make rules and regulations, and b) to enforce them.

2. **EU/UK** The Brexit decision that the UK should leave the EU may affect the existing legislation which may be changed as a consequence. How ever, as far as the following are concerned:

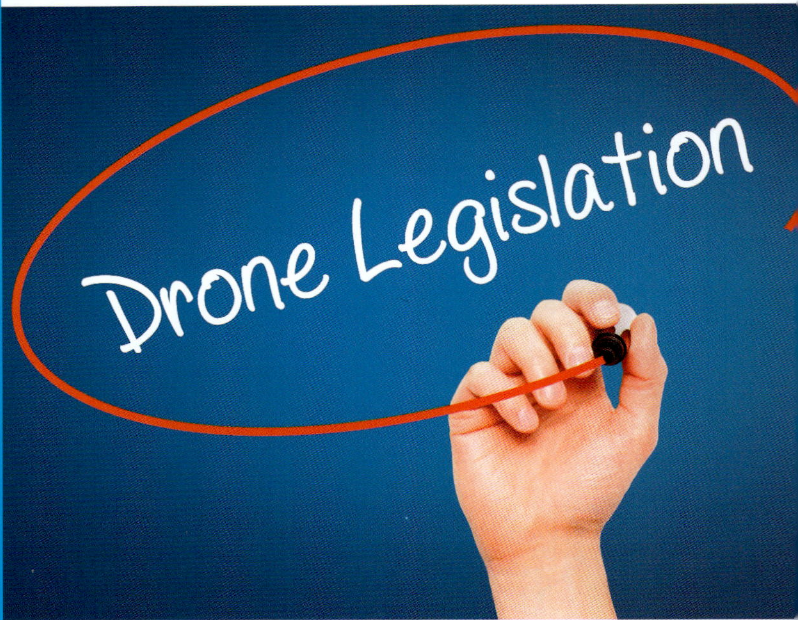

a) current EU law is embedded in UK law – at the moment the UK is likely to be fully compliant subject to agreed non-compliance. However, the EU will probably require continuing trade and new trade agreements to be based on continued compliance: agreed non-compliance may well result less access to the EU market
b) current negotiations on forthcoming EU law, eg draft EU General Data Protection Regulation - for full access to the EU market any new trade agreement the UK may result in the UK being compliant or show 'adequacy' of the UK law to the satisfaction of EU negotiations
c) future EU laws for "EU without UK" – the UK is able to ignore but if it wants new trade agreements and other project-cooperation which are related to these new EU laws, it will need to be compliant or show adequacy.
d) In the depth of the detail one knows of differences in all kinds of matters but it is not difficult to believe the EU will eventually formulate and have agreed standards for droneports, delivery corridors and literally hundreds of other drone-related topics. Will the UK be able to ignore them and expect drone trade across the Channel...?

3. **USA** A similar approach operates at a Federal level in the USA. However, each state is likely to have legislation on drones. The Drone Manufacturing Alliance has identified 270 lower level Acts – many are contradictory to others and to Federal Acts.

Lethal Miniature drone

A light-weight military drone carried by an individual which is commonly fired from a tube by released air pressure to travel by FPV to deliver a small explosive munition. The USA has a Lethal Miniature Aerial Missile Systems program (LMAMS) to further develop capability of the small loitering attack system.

Lethal Miniature drone

Drone	Comment
CH 901 (China)	• weight is 9kg • launch system is under 50kg • flight duration is 2 hours for ISR but less for munitions attack mode
Hero-30 (Israel	• operated from hand-held controller • flight duration is 30 minutes • loiters at up to 2000 feet • distance of operator from target is up to 40km • payload is 3kg
Switchblade (USA)	• operated from GCS • flight duration is 10 minutes • carries very small explosive charge • has ISR capability as alternative use

Light Detection and Ranging (LiDAR)

A technology which drones may carry where light sensors scan from the air to ultimately create 3D imagery of buildings, trees, etc for land mapping and other purposes. The images are captured as points in a three-dimensional array of grids reference points, the so-called cloud points, and portrayed as images elsewhere by various digital programs.

Light Detection and Ranging (LiDAR)

Line-of-sight operation

A flying operation with a drone during which the pilot keeps the drone in sight at all times.
Regulations require drones being used for specified purposes or operations to be kept in the pilot's line-of-sight at all times, ie within 500m: exemptions are available from the CAA. When the operator is using FPV, both the observer and the operator must follow the LOS rule and not go BLOS.
When a drone is out of the line of sight it should autonomously or manually goes into return to land (RTL) mode.

LiPo bag

A fire-protected bag made specially for carrying lithium polymer batteries.

***lithium polymer battery* (LiPo)**

A battery commonly used to power UAVs.
For safety reasons, it is recommended they are not put in place until the UAV is ready for immediate use. Similarly, batteries should be carried separately from other equipment - in a LiPo bag.

Local Government preparedness

Local governments will need to prepare for the growth of drone usage in their communities. Matters of interest are given in the table.

Local Government preparedness

Topic	Comment
Awareness and information	• members' concerns on policy and work practice • residents, businesses and visitors concerns on noise, privacy, and injury and damage • officers concerns on work practice, etc
Training and development	• identify work situations where officers will need training and development • consider needs of a) building control inspections, b) planning controls, c) housing management • needs of local employers and workforce as drone-related work arises
Economic development and employment	• develop awareness of a) local growth of drone businesses, b) education and training needs for drone-related employment
Law of drones: application	• Identify aspects of dronelaw as applied to council work, eg privacy and surveillance • Consider a) reviewing byelaws, b) contracts for employing contactors using drone services, c) insurances cover for buildings, third party liability, etc
Community resilience planning	• Coordinate any policies and practice for drones with a) police b) emergency services, d) search and rescue, e) first aid, f) local military services and g) HART
Anti-drone measures	• Consider the need for anti-drone protection of critical or sensitive assets -, a) use of geofences, b) event protection with devices to capture intrusive drones, etc

See page 13 **Byelaws**

Logbook

Commercial drone pilots should complete, but also some recreationalists will complete their logbook of operational flights and other operations. The logbook comes in two forms: 1) Manual or hardcopy, and 2) digital.

Whatever form, it is likely to have predetermined sections and part of each space may allow for customised records. Aspirants to professional status might be advised to keep a log book.
Contents are likely to include: a) date, b) times, c) UAV type and any registration details, d) flight route and places, e) purpose or mission, f) issues about the flight, g) weather, and so on.

longitudinal axis

The horizontal line from the nose to the tail of a drone.

Loon Copter

An award winning drone, Loon Copter, which has triple-environment performance capabilities, as follows:

1. take-off, hover, fly and land on land
2. land, float and move on and take off from water
3. land float, submerge, move under and emerge from water to take-off.

The developers took the first prize of $1m USD at the 2016 UAE Drones for Good Award in Dubai.

LOw-Cost Unmanned aerial vehicle Swarming Technology LOCUST

The term refers to a US Navy Office of Research project into the swarming technologies of drones.

low Earth orbit

An orbit around our planet which is above 160 km and below 2000 km; taking about 1 hour 30 minutes and about 2 hours 10 minutes respectively.
See page 83 **Spacecraft (drone)**

M

Manufacturers of drone

The global number of drone manufacturers is estimated at about 450 including about 300 making military drones.

Marine applications of drones

Several uses of at-sea drones may be listed, namely:

- counting and monitoring of sea birds
- enforcement of regulations for NOx, SOx, etc emissions from shipping in Emissions Control Areas
- inspections for damage inside of ships' hulls and other voids
- monitoring oil spills and others on water spills
- naval reconnaissance
- offshore inspections
- sea border surveillance by drone
- surveillance against drug smugglers
- surveillance against illegal fishing.

At least three countries aim to supplement maritime surveillance by aircraft with drones.
See page 16 **Coastguard – Antarctica sea ice surveillance**
Codes for drones

Marine nature reserves	Although the surveillance of marine nature reserves by the Pew Charitable Trusts under Project Eyes of the Seas is largely based on the use of satellite imagery it is being extended to use imagery from UAVs. The concerns are as follows: a) to effectively monitor the seas on a real time basis, b) to identify unusual movements of fish near marine reserves and in other seas, and c) to alert fishing authorities of illegal fishing or similar activities.
Medical, health and care	1. HARTs The Hazardous Area Response Teams (HART) of the NHS will or do have drones. The drones for the 15 medical emergency teams are supplied by the National Ambulance Resilience Unit (NARU). See page 74 **Public Safety**. 2. Defibrillators See Page 22 **Defibrillator by drone** 1 An inventor in New Zealand has installed an automated external defibrillator (AED) into a drone. 2 In the Netherlands a drone is, in effect, a defibrillator. 3. Deliveries Finally, drones are being used to deliver medicines in remote places, eg in Africa. Applications or possible applications include: • carrying blood • carrying donated organs for transplants • carrying tele-medical equipment • provision of live video broadcast to patients • sensors to detect hazardous materials, thereby warning those nearby to take precautions. See page 23 **Delivery drones**
Meteorology	Drones are used in weather forecasting as follows: a) the measurement of moisture content of the air, b) ozone measurement, c) temperature, d) warning of violent storms, and c) measurement of wind speed and direction. The subject is part of the training of drone pilots.
Micro drones (small drone)	A small or micro drone (micro unmanned aircraft systems (mUAS)) means one which has the following characteristics: a) it is made of fragile materials that break up on impact so causing little or no damage or injury, and b) weighs no more than 2kg. Cf see page 64 **Nano drones**
Migrant Offshore Aid Station (MOAS)	A surface maritime vessel supported by Schiebel S-100 camcopters based out of Malta as a marine search and rescue of migrants from Africa.

Military - Battlefield High Level Persistence Surveillance

The UK has ordered four Zephy 8, advanced high-level surveillance drones for special forces to observe and monitor communications of foe in battlefield conditions. The UAVS's characteristics are: a) function – persistent surveillance, b) operational height - 65,000 feet, c) weight - 30 kg without payload, d) payload - up to five times weight, and e) flight time - three months.

Military governance, regulation and UAVSs

Each UK military service will be subject to a hierarchy of law and governance, as indicated below in the cross references.

As far as UAVS are concerned information is subject to the Official Secrets Act unless authorised for official release. Internally, operational information and regulation is transmitted, for instance, by Defence Instructions and Notices *(DINs), eg DIN 2015DIN06-023 Regulation of remotely piloted aircraft and remotely piloted air systems.*

See page 79 **Rules of engagement (ROE) and drones**

Military advantages for UAVSs

Many countries deploy military drones but few have the capability to design and manufacture UAVSs. The MTCR (See page 104) is however partly responsible for the growth of manufacturing capability.

Military advantages for UAVSs

Like commercial applications of drones, they are increasingly seen to have advantages for military purposes. In particular drone surveillance and drone situational awareness enable missions to be accomplished in relative safety for the personnel involved. eg. USA has 93 Reapers with another 30 on ordered.

Other advantages may be discerned from the table which gives examples of "missions" for drones – relative safety, cost savings and effectiveness of outcomes are examples of their raison d'etre.

This table identifies by country several large military drones.

Large military drones

Country	Drone
China	CH-4 Shen Diao (Divine Eagle)
Iran	Shahed 129
Israel	Elbit Hermes 900
Pakistan	Burraq
Turkey	Anka Bayraktar
USA	Predator Reaper

milliAmp hours

Unit of measurement of the capacity of a battery used say, for a drone.

Mission - classification of military UAVs

UAVSs might be usefully classified according to categories of military mission. Examples of military missions for drones are shown in the table.

Thus, a concept for a new mission is followed by the choice an existing drone (or a specification for a new drone) to carry the sensors, computing paraphernalia, and other payload items needed to conduct the mission. Essentially, the UAVS rests on the correct balance of size, weight and power (SWaP) but the UAV as such is part of a *gestalt* which is the mission.

Mission - classification of military UAVSs

Mission title	Comment
'Ambulance' drone	• lifting casualties from a combat theatre (in development)
Fighter-like drone	• the combat drone such as the X-47
Meteorological drone	• gathering of weather intelligence at stratospheric height by a drone, such as Zephyr
Multi-mission drone	• the combat, etc drones in DARPA's "Gremlins" multi-outcomes program • involving a) integrated air-launch and air-recovery swarm drones, and b) expendable drone designs
Strategic ISR drone	• intelligence, surveillance and reconnaissance for the broader need, such as the RQ-4A Global Hawk
Suicide or kamikaze drone	• attack drone loaded with explosives to fly at target and hit them, so self-destructing, eg Harop, and Switchblade
surveillance drone	• battlefield surveillance, perhaps in alignment with a manned attack helicopter, being a UXV such as Shadow

(continued from previous page)

table continued from previous page

Mission title	Comment
Swarm drones	• AFRL's trial project, essentially being expendable, a strike capability for long range remote places, (USA)
Tactical ISR drone	• intelligence, persistent surveillance and reconnaissance for the combat theatre, a UAVS such as the MQ-9 Reaper, and Zephyr
Tanker drone	• a USN carrier-borne project to refuel airborne fighters

Modes

The novice pilot will need to know of and eventually be able to carry out as appropriate a number of flying "modes". Each mode is a flying sequence or pattern of flight – some are autonomous. Many are adopted or used by the pilot for a particular flight. A drone is likely to have been built with say, a dozen or so modes for flight.
The modes are numerous – a few are shown in the following table.

Modes

Mode	Description
Altitude hold	The drone reaches the set altitude and flies at that height until a change is induced. Uses include: • military autonomous drone flight to a destination • intelligence, surveillance and reconnaissance (ISR) operations
Circle	The drone flies as follows: • continuously in a circle • radius of the circle is predetermined • altitude is predetermined • nose of the drone is pointing to the centre when flying
Failsafe return	Where, if a motor is switched off or an engine fails, a flying drone will autonomously return to the launch place – the pilot at "home base" Note that if the drone has sense and avoid it should return safely: if not, it flies direct and may not avoid obstacles

table continued from previous

Mode	Description
First person view (FPV)	Flying by seeing the route through mounted front-facing camera connected either a) to goggles worn by the pilot or b) monitor screens wirelessly connected to a camera on the drone. Latency may affect the inexperienced pilot's flight. Uses include: • combat drones, eg Predator, for surveillance or missile attack • racing with a drone
Follow me	The drone which is pre-set by, for instance, an app to follow the operator pilot at a set altitude and distance. The operator should keep aware of possible obstructions in the flight path
GPS planning aka mission planning	A predetermined flight is planned using a GPS technology to set a series of waypoints. Once airborne the drone will fly autonomously along the route. Uses include: • land surveying • agricultural operations
Return home / to land	1 When a drone leaves a line-of-sight flight, in effect the drone returns and lands where the operation started 2 If commanded, the drone autonomously returns and lands at the place of take-off

modification

A change to a drone's body, component, electronic system which alters the manufacturer's drone as delivered. See page 9 **ANN**.
The change may be required in law or as a result of the manufacturer's advice. To avoid harming one's legal rights, when intending to make a modification, care should be taken to comply with any relevant terms and conditions in a valid contract, guarantee, insurance policy, warranty and the like.

Museum

In the UK no museum is known to have a permanent dedicated droneology department. There are numerous references to drones in museum-related websites.

1 **UK** Some UK museums have had exhibitions featuring drones, eg the 2016 Leonardo Da Vinci exhibition at the Science Museum, London.
2 **USA** The Hillier Aviation Museum offers drone flying lessons, build-a-drone and other events.

Drones are frequently used at archaeological sites.

Names and abbreviations for "drone"

N

The conveniently short word 'drone' is one name used more or less colloquially for technical sounding terms like:

Names and abbreviations for "drone"		
Abbreviation	Term	Comment
Not applicable	Drone/ aerial drone	• colloquial term for unmanned aerial vehicle system
RPAS	Remotely piloted aircraft system	• term which emphasises the pilot's involvement or contribution
SUAS/sUAS	Small unmanned aircraft system	• see below - here emphasis is on a small vehicle
UAV	Unmanned aerial / aircraft vehicle	• term for drone which tends to be used in official and technical contexts
UAVS	Unmanned aerial vehicle system	• term tends to emphasise the idea of a drone, controller and, in particular, the pilot, all as parts of a whole for a particular purpose or mission.

In RPAS and SUAS the word "system" is or may indicate the flyable device itself is component in a "package" of technologies used by a pilot or operator. Of the expressions UAV is probably the most common alternative to "drone" in use.

The term 'drone' is sometimes applied to robotic-like devices on land and on or under the sea, namely unmanned ground vehicles (UGVs) and unmanned marine vehicles (UMVs). The latter has examples of both surface and submersible types. Also, there is at least one drone capable of enduring all three environments.
See page 29 **"Drone"**

Nano Drones

Nano drones are exceeding small UAVs, say 10 to 20 grams and 4cm x 10cm in size. They are in use or being developed for various purposes including: a) defence purpose, eg local surveillance, and b) recreation.

Nano Drones

National Qualifying Entity (NQE)

An NQE is one of about 20 organisation in the UK which have establishments recognised by the CAA under ANO 2009 to run educational courses, training courses and practice programmes for would-be drone-crew.

ANO 2016 allows existing permissions etc but NQE staff must follow the instructions specified therein and have been ready to implement them from 25 August 2016.See page 88 **Training and assessment**

National security vetting levels

In the UK drone some work involves a degree of vetting for national security clearance, including that for the following: a) counter terrorism jobs, b) developed vetting jobs, and c) NATO jobs.
The range of positions involving drones possibly now extends to aerospace, military, nuclear and those with national critical infrastructure.
See page 81 **Security clearance** and page 105 ***Security Cleared Jobs***

National Trust policy

In the UK the National Trust has byelaws to give a blanket ban on the use of commercial and recreational drones on the heritage property. A guidance note has been issued giving an explanation of policy. The following reasons may be of interest:

- very few users have a pilot's qualification and insurance
- protection from injury or death of other visitors, staff and contractors' staff
- protection of heritage buildings and other structures from damage caused by impact of a drone
- protection of animals on National Trust land.

Where either a third party commercial organisation or a contractor employed by the National Trust wishes to use drones on or over National Trust property consent must be obtained and would be subject to the following: a) compliance with CAA regulations and requirements for drone operation, eg pilot's qualifications and experience, flight planning, and b) full range of appropriate insurance cover.

Navigation control connectivity

The navigation connectivity of a drone may be controlled by the operator by radio with for instance Bluetooth, Wifi or a satellite global positioning system (GPS).

Night flying

Flying a drone at night for recreational purposes is not allowed by the CAA; similarly for commercial flying unless consent is obtained, eg for thermal imagery. Generally, the use of thermal imagery cameras is better at night when the sun's day-heat dissipates and does not increase the temperatures of the ground and objects near to that being sought, eg a leak of steam or heat from a pipe.

In Germany, the USA and elsewhere single enterrtainment events have been held where as many as 100 drones have been flown at night at the same time.

No drone zone

An exclusion area around a building, facility or infrastructure within which drones are not allowed to enter or are grounded at all times or for a specified period.

No Fly Zone

A USA company with a UK subsidiary providing online facilities for registering property needing protection against intrusive drones, eg a nuclear power station or other critical national infrastructure.

Non-lethal weapons

Use of non-lethal weapons, particularly directed energy weapons (DEW) is becoming common. Drones are being used for their delivery, eg for crowd control. See page 28 **Directed Energy Weapons**

Nuclear radiation drone

A drone carrying radiation sensors is in development for use in a nuclear fallout incident. It will be particularly useful where the environment is hazardous for human first responders.

observer, competent	See page 18 **competent observer**
octocopter	A drone which has eight rotas.
Oil and Gas industry	UAVSs are used in the oil and gas industry. Examples are: a) oil spills at sea are sometimes monitored by drones, b) inspection of offshore platforms, eg the flare tips at a considerable cost saving on alternative use of a helicopter, and c) a drill ship inspection has been undertaken by drone -the work covered components including cranes, derrick, and helideck – instead of 17 days' work the time taken for the job was two days.
operations manual	Prepared by the pilot of a drone setting out the way in which a drone will be used and conducted in a particular commercial application. It is likely that the industry will eventually develop and adopt operational manuals for: a) standard operational procedures (SPOs), and b) emergency response plans (ERPs).
Operator	The term is defined in the ANO 2016 Article 4
Operator of a micro drone	The FAA has rules which will the pilot or operator of a micro drone. See page 1 The following characteristics are incorporated: • the "operator" would be the person flying the vehicle • he or she would be at least 17 years of age • the operator would be "qualified" by passing an "aeronautical knowledge test" • the operator would need a "FAA UAS operator certificate" and maintain it every two years by further knowledge tests • the operator would not need to have medicals or a private pilot license.
Ordnance Survey plan making	Ordnance Survey (OS), the UK's national mapping agency, has trialled some commercial drones for its work. The OS also monitors technological developments in the stability of drones for map-work as well as the improvements in mounted technological instruments.
Organ donation transport	1. **USA** It is understood that trials in the USA are planned to deliver organ donations by drone in a tie-up between the Chinese company EHang and Lung Biotechnology. The 184 Drone is the proposed vehicle for the service. The tag MOTH – Manufactured Organ Transport Helicopter denotes the scheme. 2. **India** The Indian the National Design and Research Forum (NDRF) is developing a UAVS and systems for transporting transplant organs which includes: • payload of say, 250gms • container a) standard organ transport container, or b) a device which will preserve the organ

- range of 100km – presumably a longer range would be possible with droneport hubs for battery changes
- regard is needed for the duration of preservation – which varies and can be range from 10 to 25 hours depending on the kind of organ.

Over-crowd flying

Safety has been an ongoing concern for the drone industry. Generally, the FAA and other regulators have regulated over-crowd flying. However, within the *Pathfinder Program* (see below) the FAA has initiated trials into flying over crowds. The evaluations are awaited.

Packstation

P

DHL's *Parcelcopter Skyport* is example, being an unmanned shed-like container of fully automated equipment able to take a customer's parcel, deposit it in a container which is then fitted into a delivery drone – *Parcelcopter*. The container is, in effect, part of the drone's body. When the drone is not in use it is effectively housed in a roof-top hanger part of the packstation.
The drone delivers the parcel to another packstation where the recipient collects it by dialling in a code on the keypad fixed near the closed door of the deposit box.
All of the operations are automated, even the closing of the roof panels to create the secure hanger.

Pathfinder Focus Areas

In the USA this is a FAA program of projects to consider how certain UAVS concerns should be addressed. The work is commissioned by the FAA and undertaken by industry companies and / or universities. The projects are instituted using *cooperative research and development agreements* (CRDAs).

Payload

A drone's cargo, if any, and any add-on technological equipment, eg a camera.

Permission for Aerial Work (PFAW)

A CAA document, entitled *Permission for Aerial Work* (PFAW), is a statutory requirement before a person may fly a drone for paid commercial operations in the UK. Applicants must follow a recognised training and assessment at an approved establishment before a permission document is issued. See ANO 2016 Article

person in charge

The individual who pilots or operates the UAV. The term is fully defined, for example, in the CAA document *ANO 2009.ORS4 No 1168, General Exemption E4185 Small unmanned aircraft - First person view (FPV) flying* of 28 April 2016. (To be read with ANO 1016 from 25 August 2016)
Cf See page 18 ***competent observer***

Pest control (pilots in command*)

The control of pests in difficult or dangerous conditions may be avoided with safety, eg without ladders by using drones as follows: a) examining hard-to-reach areas, such trees, roof gutters and parapets for nests, b) locating nests of wasps, hornets and the like, and c) spraying pesticides onto them.

Photography

See page 5 **Aerial filming and photography with a drone**
See page 89 **Warp imagery**

Pipeline inspections

Pipeline grids have extensive distances which would involve much staff travel. Drones offer a means of low-cost, low-resource inspection of relatively short duration.
A drone, *Buildrone*, was the winner of an award at the *Drones for Good Award in the UAE*. It is designed for inspecting and repairing leaking pipelines by spaying the holed pipeline with liquid polyurethane foam which expands to seal the break.

Pilot training

1. **UK** A commercial drone pilot is licenced by the CAA after attending and passing a training course at a qualified national entity (QNE). The syllabus is likely to include:

- airmanship • airspace and operations • drone operations manual
- flight – planning and operations • flight - principles and practice
- law and drones • LiPo • meteorology • navigation
- observer's responsibilities • pilot's/operator's responsibilities
- risk assessment • privacy.

2. **USA** From 29 August 2016 would-be commercial drone pilots must comply with Part 107, including: a) pass a knowledge test at one of nearly 700 testing centres, b) obtain a remote pilot's certificate (but not a manned pilot's licence), c) be 16 years or older, and d) pass a Transportation Security Administration vetting. (Please note Part 107 has 647 pages!)

pilot's eye	When flying in first person view, the perspective of the person in charge as seen through the drone's on-board camera and video goggles or other device used.
pitch	In drone terminology the term has the following meanings: • When flying or stationary in the air, a tilt movement so that drone comes away from the level or current angle of its body's front-rear axis or nose heading. • When flying or hovering, a fixed angle at which the body of the drone is angled to the horizontal plane. When a quadcopter is flying the pitch is created or altered by a change in the speed of the front or rear pairs of rotors.
platform	A military term and sometimes commercial term used particularly when referring to an actual physical drone as being suitable for one or more particular kinds of mission system or commercial function.
Police service applications	In the UK increasing numbers of the police forces deploy drones in numerous contexts. Kent Police have used a drone for about two years working with police forces in continental Europe for Border control activities. (Similarly, in the USA drones are increasingly being deployed by police and other enforcement agencies.) Generally, police forces have used or are looking into the use of drones for: • armed patrols • assessments of airport security • barricaded suspects • bomb incidents • crime scene photography and documentation • crowd control • disaster response • EOD missions • fire incidents • hazardous materials (HAZMAT) responses • hostage rescue • hunting and capturing drones being used for criminal purposes • investigations of road traffic collisions • motorway traffic surveillance • public safety • sieges involving armed persons • surveillance at sea and control of the national border • search and rescue missions - for missing persons, animals, etc in the open country or wilderness • surveillance at protests.

In the USA the need for some State police force to obtain a warrant to use drones in criminal investigations is enacted or under consideration by Federal or state legislators. However, it is likely that search and rescue, hostage situations and certain other operations are or would be exempt.

Police surveillance

As mentioned above a number of UK police forces use drones for various functional operations. Furthermore the EU is reported to be developing a regime of drones for police surveillance operations.
See page 57 **Marine Applications of Drones**

Political and regulatory concerns

1. Legislators and regulators have or will have to address the following concerns about the use of drones:
- traceability of drone owners, pilots, etc.
- public safety for citizens, eg against aerial attacks with hazardous substances and weaponry by drones
- protection of critical national infrastructure and local infrastructure
- protection of the privacy of individuals and organisations
- development of a sustainable industry, eg operations and emergency
- concerns about the military uses of drones
- regulation and enforcement of the use and application of drones in particular sectors of the economy - commercial and leisure
- education, training, licensing and assessment of pilots and other staff who will be using drones including organisations for training
- operational restrictions on height, distance from non-participants, building and structures, weight of the vehicle, weight of load, pilot competence.

2. The UK has an All Party Parliamentary Group on Drones (APPG) which examines governments' uses of drones for all purposes.

Postal services

Postal services in a) Finland, b) Qatar and c) Switzerland are proposing to use drones to deliver mail eg to remote villages in the mountains in Finland and Switzerland.

power driven

In byelaws and other public estate documents, the term is sometimes given to mean the likes of *motored engines driven by the combustion of petroleum vapours or similar materials.*
See page 13 **Byelaws**

Power sources

Battery power is the usual source for most commercial, hobbyist, racing and recreational drones. However, the Danish engineering consultancy, COWI, has used cable power for a continuous monitoring in a traffic management study. The weight limited the height of observations to 65 to 70 metres.
The Zephyr UAVS is an example of solar-powered drone used for ISR and weather forecasting at stratospheric heights.
See page 37 **Fuel**

Practice notes

Lloyds Register have produced guidance notes on the use of drones in certain work situations. Similarly, a profession may prepare and issue best practice notes – sometimes they are mandatory or are guidance. So far as is known nothing has been made available in the UK on drones in work contexts.
See page 104 **Lloyds Register**

Predator

A large unmanned combat aerial vehicle (UCAV) used for ISR and weapon attacks by flying in remote split operations. For long flights the Predator can be flown autonomously. A 24-hours patrol requires four drones and about 450 personnel.
A relatively slow UCAV, the Predator is not suited to be deployed where there is anti-aircraft fire or air-to-air attack by manned aircraft. It was first used in Bosnia in 1995.
See page 61 **Mission - classification of military UAVs**
See page 78 ***remote split operations***

Printable drones

In 2017 the US Army is to test "On-Demand Small Unmanned Aircraft Systems" or printable drones. The aim is that in a combat zone the printed parts would be made and off-the-shelf electronic components would be assembled with them to make drones. This is intended as an as-and-when the need arises weapon or surveillance system.

Privacy

Drones have added new concerns about personal and corporate privacy. A drone either with a camera capable of taking still or moving images or with first person view technology may breach privacy.
Similarly, without permission of the property owner's a drone may be used to fly inside that person's building or enclosure - with the intention of the crew either to take unauthorised images or to view the layout or contents, perhaps for criminal purposes. Points from various countries are as follows:

1. **France**: Since early 2016 any persons who are under surveillance by drone must be informed by the drone operators
2. **UK**: Any lawfully obtained images should be kept securely and used in accord with the data principles under schedule 1 of the Data Protection Act 1998
3. **USA**: The National Telecommunications Information Administration has led a stakeholders' review of privacy and drones. The DMA welcomes many aspects of the outcomes but is concerned that drone users need to meet higher standards to obtain data than the standards imposed on users of other technologies collecting the same data.

propeller

1. A hub with two or more radiating aerofoil blades which is fitted, in the first instance, to the horizontal shaft of a fixed-wing drone's motor to provides the forward drive for lift-off or movement for flying; or

propeller guard

secondly, to the tail of a drone helicopter to prevent uncontrolled rotation of the same. Cf See page 79 ***rotor***

2. As "props" a term used to refer or denote any drone's propellers / rotors.

propeller guard

A fitting around each of a drone's propellers so as to afford protection against injury or damage in the event of a drone hitting a person or obstruction.
Sometimes the airframe or body of the drone is shaped to afford a similar function.
See page 42 **Indoor flying and in enclosed spaces**

Protection

1 **Clothing** Despite accidents being reported there is little literature of protective clothing although employers in the UK may find both health and safety legislation and the terms and conditions for commercial business insurance expect regard for such clothing.
Online sources suggest or recommend specific items of protective clothing which may be suitable for drone work.
Regard might therefore be had to: a) helmets with visors, b) safety goggles or spectacles, c) hi-Vis jackets or gilets, d) non-slash or non-cut garments, e) gloves, trousers and other garments (similar to chain-saw items), f) boots, trousers etc (similar to forestry boots).

2. **Equipment** As far as equipment is concerned items such as a) high barrier fencing b) catch-nets may afford protection to spectators and others. Similarly, on-board sensors such as return to home and sense and avoid would add to the protection of all.

3. **Cybersecurity** The need to embed cybersecurity protection against hacking will come to be more widely recognised as buyers become more aware of the need to protect against cyber vulnerabilities. Testing against hacking is conducted in netted enclosures as a protection against runaway drones affected by hacking tests.

pseudo-satellite, high altitude

A drone with satellite-like characteristics in that it flies at high altitude for long periods.
See page 92 **Zephyr**

Public safety

Drones are used after accidental or terrorist incidents or threats involving hazardous materials (HAZMAT). Such emergencies might be biological, chemical, nuclear or radiological which may be monitored with drones by the accident and emergency services in relative safety.
See page 58 **Medical, health and care**

Q

quadcoptor A drone with four rotors.

Racing drones

R

Drones are becoming popular for racing sport- both indoors and outside. The unmanned aerial vehicle system for racing includes: a) a drone with a front facing camera, b) a controller used by the racing contestant pilot, c) a set of goggles with two antennae, and d) a software package enables first person view through the goggles.
Speeds of up to say 80 mph are achievable and skill needs to be developed to deal with a slight latency.
See page 12 ***Brain controlled interface***
See page 102 ***British FPV Racing Association***

Railway industry

UAVs might be used in railways, such as for: a) route planning and design, b) seeking encroachments of vegetation, and c) analysing and modelling slopes for landslip and flood.
Examples of work on railways include:

1. **India** Indian Railways is developing an R&D group to improve railways in the country. An early project will be to research the use of drones carrying geo-spatial technologies to monitor performance on numerous railway projects, eg the *Dedicated Freight Corridor.*

2. **USA** Under the FAA Pathfinder Program, BNSF Railroad are exploring the use of UAVS to examine rail system infrastructure for damage etc.

Raptors

See page 20 **Countermeasures against drones**

ready to fly (RTF)

A drone which is boxed with all its parts supplied.
Cf page 9 ***almost ready to fly***

real time

Essentially, the present moment or "at this instance", but in drone flying this is subject to any latency in the system being used.
Generally real time may not be required where data has to be analysed but in some situations it may possibly be important, such as: a) in accident and emergency, b) in searching for missing persons, c) in military combat, and d) in surveillance for capture.
Cf page 49 **latency**

Recreational and sports usage

Concerns about the misuse of drones by recreational and sports users include ensuring that they are flown properly and safely. To this end, the use of websites and social media platforms are being or will be used by the police and other bodies to inform the public.
Restrictions in different international jurisdictions vary but include the following for recreational purposes:

- join an approved or designated club which has been accredited by the authority – for insurance, safety and security reasons
- take heed of any club benefits or seek commercial offerings on insurance, training programmes, organised practice sessions and the like
- join training programmes and undertake practice sessions – essentially to learn basic stages of flying and to develop command and control competencies
- some equipment, such as cameras, laser devices, are prohibited in some jurisdictions on security or privacy grounds
- when flying a) keep the drone within the line of sight, b) keep below a certain height, c) operate only in daylight, and d) in good weather conditions

- also only fly outside specified kilometre distances of airports and other zones and keep away from individuals, crowds, houses, factories and other buildings
- do not carry out operations for commercial purposes without permission of the regulatory body.

red line corridor

A designated route for small cargo drones, essentially for medical and emergency use, often in remote locations, eg Africa.

Registration

Several countries require the registration of drones. As yet there is no known international convergence of registration requirements between countries. Examples are given as follows:

- **Bahamas:** From 2 February 2016 drones must be registered; all imported drones must be registered; and the owner is required to obtain a certificate of registration before it is released by the Customs Department.
- **China:** China announced drone registration on a trial basis early in 2016.
- **India:** Registration not required under draft guidelines
- **Ireland:** Registration has been required from 21December, 2015. Ireland was first to require online drone registration.
- **Kenya:** Stakeholders' meetings are arranged to review and develop regulatory framework for UAVs by 2017.
- **UK:** Registration is not required as yet.
- **USA:** Registration is required - the FAA has registered some 0.5m owners of drones by June 2016..
  The FAA has warned that unregistered owners should not need the help-for-a-fee of an online "registration company".

Regulatory bodies

Examples of regulatory bodies for drones themselves are shown in the table. Other regulators in a particular country may have concerns about cybersecurity, defence, privacy, military aviation, security and surveillance. Many regulatory regimes are in early development with changes in the pipeline or pronouncements expected in the near future.

Regulatory bodies

Country	Regulator	Comment
Ireland	Irish Aviation Authority	• Registration required for drones over 1 kg • At May 2016 some 14 organisations were reported online as being registered

table continued from previous

Country	Regulator	Comment
India	Directorate General of Civil Aviation (DGCA)	• Guidelines published as draft • Sale of a drone requires consent
Kenya	Kenya Civil Aviation Authority	• Regulations published in draft • Categories of drones are commercial, recreational and sports
Rwanda	Rwanda Civil Aviation Authority (RCAA)	• As at February 2016, drone regulations were understood to be in draft
South Africa	South African Civil Aviation Authority RCAA) (SACAA)	• Comprehensive regulations have operated from 1 July 2015 • Commercial pilots must hold a licence • Commercial flights must be backed with five authorisations • Flying covered by no fly zones and other requirements
Uganda	Uganda Aviation Authority	• Cameraships must not be imported into Uganda
UK	Civil Aviation Authority (CAA)	• Regulates commercial and recreational drones. • Works closely with European Aviation Safety Agency. • Rules published, aka Dronecode • Registration not yet required • Review of UK drone strategy under way

table continued from previous

Country	Regulator	Comment
USA	Federal Aviation Administration (FAA)	• Registration required - some 0.5 million (June 2016) by online report • New rules published by FAA - Part 107 which is due to operate from 25 August 2016 • Commercial operations require approval • Pathfinder Program has projects to develop commercialisation of drones

"Regulation" for aid

For about five years international aid agencies and their associated emergency services have been using drones in the aftermath of natural and other disasters. The drone work has sometimes been in countries which had no regulations for drones.
More recently moves have been made establishing model regulations, rules or code for the use of drones in delivering international aid following natural disasters and in war zones.

***remote split operations* (RSO)**

A military term to denote the dual but separate functions whereby one team launch and land (recover) a drone by line-of-sight flying; and, once airborne, the second team's pilot a) flies the drone by first person view, and b) sets autonomous flying parameters. The sensor operator controls the target pod for surveillance and combat targeting purposes.
See page 39 ***ground control station***

Remotely piloted aircraft (RPA)

The term 'remotely piloted aircraft' is usually used and preferred to 'unmanned aerial vehicle' or 'drone 'by service personnel – it does indicate that flying and attack decisions are made or set up by humans rather than by an autonomous robotic machine.

Repair plan

At least one manufacturer in the USA offers a repair plan for selected drones. They cover repairs and replacement parts for specified periods and are subject to exclusions.
If the drone is sold the policy benefits, which is linked to the FAA registration details, passes to the new owner.

***return to land / home mode* (RTL)**

The flying sequence of a drone which is autonomous or the operator adopts when a drone leaves the line-of-sight. In effect the drone returns and lands where the operation started.

reverse engineering	Electronic and mechanical engineering process from concept; through design, perhaps adaptive; building; and trialling a drone. For instance,all this by the use of a procured or captured drone.
Road building	Drones have been used to measure the need for construction materials for roads. Camera and other sensors take data of the sizes of excavations and perhaps embankment volumes. Afterwards at base analytical techniques are used to give the requirements.
rogue drone	A UAV used for a criminal or anti-social purpose.
roll	When a drone is flying, a movement of partial or complete rotation along the lateral, longitudinal or vertical axis. See page 11 **barrel roll**
rotor	A hub with two or more radiating aerofoil blades which is fitted to the vertical shaft of a helicopter or multi-rotor drone's motors to provides the forward drive for lift-off or movement for flying. The term "props" is often used to refer to a drone's rotors. Cf page 72 **propeller**
Royal Air Force	By 2030 the RAF is likely to a about one third of its aircraft as UAVS with a variety of mission capabilities partly under the Future Combat Air Systems (FCAS). This is being, it is understood, partly worked up with France - although Brexit may require it to be tweaked..? At present the RAF has UAVs including Reaper, Protector, with the Future Combat Air System in development and the Zephyr in production, etc.
Royal Navy and drones	1. **Notification of intention to fly** Police in Devon and Cornwall has informed drone users that they must inform the Royal Navy (RN) of any intention to fly a drone in the counties. A three-fold purpose is behind the requirement: • avoiding collision with low flying RN aircraft • alerting RN security personnel about the flying • forewarning information to fit with countermeasure against illicit photography or terrorist actions. 2. **No Drone Zones (NDZ)** The Royal Navy's establishments are designated as no drone zones. 3. **Inspection of warships** Drones are being trialled to inspect warships for maintenance purposes.
Rules of engagement (ROE) and drones	The rules of engagement are military instructions, aka laws, protocols, etc, describing how particular operations in a war, eg with drones, are to be

properly carried out, essentially what are not acceptable actions or activities. For instance in the USA, ROE must be observed by UAV military pilots during operations, as governed - for example – by rules of engagement protocols for the chain of command from the occupants of a GCS to the President. (See: page 100 – for reference to M T McCurley with K Maure.)

For a particular country, any ROE are distinguishable in sovereign and international law from the international "rules of war" and any "rules for the use of force".

Rules for the use of force (RUF)

Where applicable by a state, briefly, the rules of force govern the operational conduct of military personnel and armed civilian guards, in for instance, a civil disturbance, a maritime attack on a ship. If UAVSs are used by these personnel, their operators need to observe RUF.

Rules of war

An internationally recognised body of law governing the conduct of military operations in accord with fairness and recognition of rights, eg human rights, which protects all but particularly civilians, such as children, women and elderly persons.

runway independence

Descriptive of some aircraft including drones with VTOL technology propulsion systems which enables the avoidance of need for a runway.

Safety

In manned aviation safety is a part of the system of protocols for our global safety-based industry. By contrast, for many nations the UAVS industry has something of a "safety gap" which is being addressed in both commercial and non-commercial sectors.
See page 103 **European Aviation Safety Agency**

1. Non-commercial users

Generally, for recreationists and some users of non-commercial UAVs, the safety criteria are based on a) a loosely promoted set of flying rules, b) line-of-sight mode and c) learning by doing approaches - generally without formal tuition. See page 22 **Data...etc flight insurance**

2. Commercial users

For the commercial sector safety is being developed with or by a) pilot training to national standards, b) formal authorisation of businesses by national aviation bodies, c) standardised operational procedures (SOPs), d) emergency response plans (ERPs), and e) flight planning.
ANO 2016 sets out a range of requirements, including:

a) Article 241 and 242 set out the obligations concerning endangering safety of persons and property by negligent, reckless and permitting behaviours.
b) Article 94 and aircraft sets out safety and other matters for small unmanned aircraft.
c) Article 95 sets out safety and other matters for small unmanned surveillance aircraft.
See Part 1

Satellites and certain drones	Satellites and certain other drones, eg Zephyr, have similar surveillance functions so comparison is worthwhile. A drone has the following advantages: a) relatively much less costly to create and to run, b) image resolution is better – as low as a few centimetres, c) avoids obscure ground imagery by operating beneath clouds, and d) enable local groups to develop and possess ownership of their own data sets.
Sea ice conditions	Resupply icebreaker ships travelling to McMurdo Station have used drones to spot routes in difficult sea ice conditions. The use of drones has meant aircraft were not needed so personnel were not at risk of their lives. The drone used was a Puma AE drone with the following features: a) flight duration – 3.5 hours, b) range - nearly 10 miles, c) weight - 13.5 pounds.
Search and rescue	The use of drones for search and rescue is catching on. In Japan a robot dog (UGV) has been trialled for investigating collapsed buildings. Possible use of drones in the UK by Kent Fire and Rescue Service (KFRS) and Kent Search and Rescue (KSAR) may come about. In Switzerland algorithms have been developed from 20,000 photographs to enable drones with an artificial intelligence unit to track paths in forests and mountains.
Security clearance	1. **UK** Working in UAVSs industries may require clearance in accord with the levels of clearance for national security. The drone jobs needing such clearance are likely to include those involving personnel in positions in the military, government, research, design and development and aviation. See page 105 Security Cleared Jobs. 2. **USA** Would-be commercial operators are vetted by the Transportation Security Administration under Part 107. See page 105 **Security Ceared Jobs**
segregated airspace	Airspace which is reserved for a particular purpose, eg a drone delivery corridor, and therefore not available to others.
Selective Availability Anti-Spoofing Module	The Selective Availability Anti-Spoofing Module (SAASM) is a US military countermeasure against the spoofing of drones.
sense and avoid	A technology whereby a flying drone detects autonomously another object in its flight path and takes action to move away from it, thus preventing damage or destruction
Sensor	1 A unit containing the apparatus which senses and measures some environmental or other effect. 2 A system linked to a sensor or more than one sensor by wireless connectivity or wiring so as to collect, store, perhaps analyse and transmit output from the data produced by the sensors.

Sensors carried by Drones

The list of possible sensors embedded in or mounted on a UAVS is often substantial and will depend on the drone's missions or functions. Important sensors will be needed for the flying modes or working the drone itself, such as a) accelerometer, b) barometer, c) gyroscope, d) magnetometer, e) optical flow, and f) sonar.
Other sensors will be related to the mission or function of the drone as a platform for carrying sensors, computers and other equipment; the mission will be IRS, land surveying and so on.

Shares

There are a few quoted companies making drones or drone-related products and services. Examples are:

1. **France** The Euronet Paris stock exchange has a) Delta Drone SA and b) Parrott SA.
2. **USA** NASDAQ has a) AeroVironment (AVAV) manufactures UAVs, b) Drone Aviation Holding Corp (OTC: DRNE) makes and tests tethered drones and aerostat systems, and c) GoPro Inc (NASDAQ: GPRO) is manufacturing drones and imagery equipment.

Sheep

In Norway searching for lost sheep in rural and perhaps mountainous areas is being conducted with drones. Infrared cameras are mounted on the drone and scan the area for sources of body heat from the sheep. The sheep might otherwise be hidden from view – masked by snow or hidden under bushes. A drone owner has demonstrated the rounding up of a flock of sheep.

shell

Component of a drone which is usually colourful for visual recognition which encloses the drone's body, so affording some protection. (The ID number, if any, is usually placed on the case.)

shielded operation	So-called in New Zealand, a shielded operation is "a flight within 100m of an object that is capable of stopping it". New Zealand's regulatory framework, particularly Part 101 and the Advisory Circular, give guidance on flying shielded operations at night and in otherwise restricted areas
Small unmanned aircraf	For ANO 2016 Schedule 2 etc this means any unmanned aircraft not more than 20kg without fuel but including equipment, etc. Cf see page 90 **Weight**
Smartphone by drone	A so-called "phonedrone", ie a drone which carries a smartphone, has been developed by SenseLab to be carried by the itinerant user. In an emergency the drone may be used in several ways: • where the user needs medicine, the device will travel to a predetermined pharmacy for the medicine and carry it back to the user • where the user lacks mobile phone coverage, eg in wilderness conditions – the phonedrone will seek out a mobile station and transmit messages to call assistance • where the user is lost the phonedrone will fly to search for a way and signpost it • in an emergency event, eg earthquake, the phonedrone will record information from above and transmit it to predetermined recipients, eg emergency units.
Solar powered drone	A drone fitted with solar panels as a source of electrical power to drive the motor propulsion system. Such drones, eg Zephyr, have the following advantages: • relatively light weight • less costly to operate • airborne for relatively long periods • able to operate at very high altitudes. Uses include: • intelligence, surveillance and reconnaissance (ISR) operations • storm watching • collection of weather data.
Spacecraft (drone)	DARPA is contracting Boeing to create a re-useable hypersonic XS-1 drone-like spacecraft to deploy military and commercial satellites around our planet in low-Earth-orbit. The drone could be aimed to be deployed 10 times in 10 days at a cost of $5 million a time to carry a payload of up to 5,000 pounds satellites.
Special Drawing Rights	A reserve bundle of currencies in various proportions - dollar, euro, pound sterling and yen – used, for instance, in international trade and in insurance cover. See page 43 **Insurance law for drones**

spoofing	The act of generating GPS navigation signals which enables the spoofer to take over an unprotected drone by overriding the pilot's weaker, unencrypted or jammed command signals. See page 46 **Jamming**
Sports and recreation drones	Most regulatory jurisdictions make the distinction between drones for commercial use and those for use for sports and recreation sometimes referred to as "hobbyist drones". On 4 May 2016 in the USA the FAA issued a Memorandum entitled *Educational use of unmanned aerial systems* which included interpretive information about education use but also about hobby and recreational drone usage. Using drones for sports are regulated in the usual way but in some countries there are special requirements. For instance, in Kenya drones flown for sports purposes must be done so within a club setting. Third party insurance must be held by the owner of the drone. The sports club needs to be registered with the KCAA. See page 43 **Insurance law for drones**
Spraying with drones	In rural and wild areas it is likely that spraying will soon be by drones. Subject to regulatory requirements, possible applications include: a) parks and open spaces to control weed infestation, eg Japanese knotweed, and b) hills and mountains to clear bracken.
Standards	See page 32 **EU standards for drones**
Standard 802.11	The IEEE standard which determines acceptable or compliant WiFi products, being products which are used on any of the internet's Wireless Local Area Network.
Structure from Motion (Sfm)	A photogrammetry technology used in surveying areas of land.
suicide drone	A UAV which carries an explosive device and is deliberately flown into an enemy position and set off.
Surveillance	See page 15 **Camera Surveillance – certification** See page 16 **Coastguard – Antarctica sea ice surveillance** See page 59 **Military - Battlefield High Level Persistence Surveillance** See page 71 **Police Surveillance** See Page 84 **Surveillance Camera Code of Practice**
Surveillance Camera Code of Practice	For the England and Wales, a code of 12 guiding principles on surveillance by camera prepared and published by the Surveillance Camera Commissioner. Any person or organisation carrying out surveillance

photography by drone, CCTV cameras and other means must comply by using their devices in a manner which is proportionate, transparent and effective. See page 15 **Camera Surveillance – Certification**

swarm drone

Swarm drone is another collective name for a drone which has the capability of flying or floating in a large number and interacting on some collective purpose with or without human intervention.

A sea-based swarm drone has been developed by the two institutes in Portugal, namely, the Institute of Telecommunications at University Institute of Lisbon and the University of Lisbon. Their small flotilla swarm of 10 drones demonstrated capability of tasks including the following: a) aggregation, b) dispersion, c) monitoring an area, d) navigation to a waypoint.

systems integrator

The individual or team with the role and activities of building a UAVS to a specification will seek to integrate sensors and other components so that the system will achieve the desired outcomes at the optimum SWaP for the budget.

T

Tanker drone

See page 6 **aerial tanker drone**

Taxation

This item is designed to alert readers to taxes which may arise in respect of UAVs. It is in no way comprehensive but merely indicates that there may be a need to take the possible payments of one or more taxes into account when budgeting a project for commercial or recreational purposes.

Taxation

Country	Comment
India	• Passengers entering India with a drone is likely to face a demand for some kind of import duty.
UK	• See page 42 Inheritance tax liability
USA	**Minesotta** • Drone owners pay sales tax and tax for use. **Nevada** • incentives and abatements from various taxes so as to encourage investment in the state's aviation industry, including drones

"Taxi -like" drone

In trials the China's EHang 184 carries a person of up to 100kg. It is said to be the basis for a future offering of taxi-like service. Travelling autonomously for just over 20 minutes at 60mph, it is likely to be used in relatively unpopulated areas.

Technology applications

A drone is usually capable of carrying a payload comprising one or more technological devices. Applications of the on-board technologies are likely to be through a network with autonomous control communications or control by the operator or colleagues.
The following technologies are identified:

- acoustic sensors to identify and track intrusive drones
- infrared search and tracking
- high-performance electro-optical/infrared (EO/IR) camera – for instance used for military ISR operations
- LiDAR See page 55 **Light Detection and Ranging**
- non-kinetic electronic attack equipment allowing capture or destroy
- radar
- technology allowing operations without interfering with friendly operations by others
- thermal imaging cameras, eg for search and rescue. See page 87 **Thermal imaging camera**

telemetry

A technology which enables the pilot to receive data about the drone's flight such as a) altitude, b) battery's remaining capacity, c) climb, d) direction, e) location GPS, f) pitch, g) roll, g) yaw, etc.

Telescopic drone

A USA patent (No. 3703998 A 1972) covers an air launched drone with telescopic fuselage and aerofoil components. The purpose envisaged enables air launches of relatively large drones.
A mother aircraft with a small cargo hold carries the compacted telescopic drone. The drone is launched by being a) dropped from the hold on a frame, b) unfurled, and c) released to fly.

test site

Generally a place for testing drones or evaluating a technological device or a system mounted on a drone. Both UK and USA have them.
Examples to indicate the range of test work are shown in the table on page 87

testing centre knowledge

One of 693 places in the USA where applicants for Part 107 are tested on their knowledge.

Test sites	
Test site	Work
Nevada	• standards for air traffic
New York Griffiss International Airport	• integrated manned and unmanned flying in crowded skies
Texas Texas A&M University	• airworthiness and safety
Virginia	• aspects of risk

Thermal imaging camera

A drone's mounted device for sensing and photographing losses of heat from a) animals, b) humans, c) smouldering fires, and d) other sources.
The technology may best be used at night and in hazy or opaque scenarios. It is particularly useful for the following: a) in law enforcement, hunt and capture of miscreants and escaped wild animals, b) leakage loss of heat or steam from a building's pipes, c) search, etc operations, eg missing person.
See page 91 **Wildfires**

throttle

Component by which the pilot may change the speed of the rotor motors – thereby changing speed in a horizontal direction and also to give the drone lift or descent (the angle of the rotor blades are changed for this purpose).

toy grade

Descriptive of a drone with flying capability based on a minimum of technologies, being suitable for children or first-time basic learners. Use at an early stage will avoid damage of loss of a more sophisticated or expensive UAV.

Toy grade

Training and assessment

Many commercial business and public services will need staff to be trained to fly a drone. An credited course is likely to include the following syllabus:
- law of drones • logbooks • crew roles and activities • pre-flight inspections and checks • creation and or use of operations manuals
- maintenance of and servicing of vehicle • eye / hand coordination for flying • methodology for in flying practice for the line of sight
- flight patterns and manoeuvers • risk assessment and flight safety
- operation of devices for eg. camera and video photography
- flight assessments for stated purposes
- weather conditions and interpretation for unmanned flight.

However there are two aspects to training:
1 Training to become a competent commercial pilot, eg Part 107 or UK BNUC equivalent
2. Training to gain a skill or competence in some application, eg tower in spections, search and rescue.

transit zone

A transit zone is one defined in statute, regulation, etc which empowers a drone operator to fly in airspace but no higher than a prescribed height from ground level.
See page 76 **red line corridor**

transmitter

A term sometimes used to mean controller.

tricoptor

A drone which has three rotors.
See page 29 **drone**

turning

A partial rotation to left or right is a turn on the yaw or vertical axis. A continuous yaw is a spinning movement about the vertical.

UK Airprox Board

See page 101 **Air Prox Board, UK**

uncontrolled airspace

U

Airspace which is not controlled airspace and in which the main users are military aircraft, commercial and private aircraft, balloons, unmanned aerial vehicles (UAVs) and the like aircraft. This airspace may be zoned, etc.
Cf page 18 ***controlled airspace***

Unmanned Aerial Systems Traffic Management (UTM)

In the USA, a NASA project of collaborative investigation and action is likely to result in policies and practice for the traffic management of UAVs.

unmanned tactical aerial platform (UTAP)

A fighter-like long range drone with a jet engine which flies at 50,000ft carrying a payload of about 160kg (known as UTAP-22).

unmanned aerial vehicle (UAV)

A technical term for 'drone'.

unmanned aerial vehicle system (UVAS)

A technical term for a drone which tends to emphasise the drone, controller and, in particular, the pilot; all as parts of a whole.

USA Government use of drones

The government of the USA uses drones for a number of purposes, including: a) border monitoring, b) managing Federal land holdings, c) wildfire monitoring, d) supporting law enforcement agencies, e) surveillance and combat operations, f) training military personnel.

Warehouse stock control

Walmart (USA) are to use drones in warehouses to control stock by taking images of stock and analysing them. Data will enable restocking and correcting errors of wrongly placed stock.

warp imagery

A photographic form of art imagery where a series of photographs of a view, eg part of a city, are taken, for instance, by cameradrone from different altitudes and subsequently digitally stitched to create a three dimensional effect.

W

waypoint

A virtual place or position on land or at sea which is a map referenced point, being of use to navigators to verify their position.
An drone may be programmed with a series of waypoints for an autonomous or self-steered journey.

Weather

A drone has an optimal performance in good weather which will deteriorate with deteriorating weather. The main weather influences are wind and rain. Generally, recreational drones and many commercial drone applications require wind to be less than 25 knots. Also, heavy rain may prevent or stop flying.
In less inclement windy weather but gusty, the presence of animals, crowds, heritage buildings, and trees may prevent full performance.
See page 102 **Aviation Digital Data Service**
See page 37 ***gimbal***

Weather forecast

Before leaving home base to go flying the pilot may need to check the weather forecast for the area in which the intended flight will take place. Avoid weather which is beyond the UAV's limits or capabilities.

Weed eradication

Drones have been used to identify and quantify areas of weed infected land, eg along river banks. One drone-based project in the UK dealt with the following weeds: a) giant hogweed, b) Himalayan balsam, c) Japanese knotweed, and d) rhododendron.
In Australia a large drone carrying 20 litres of herbicide has been used to eradicate large areas of blackberry on steep slopes.

Weight

For regulatory purposes drones tend to be categorised by reference to weight and\ or their mission or function. For instance, the draft regulations (April 2016) for UAVs in India give four weight categories, namely:

1. **Micro:** Under 2kg Cf page 64 **Nano Drone**
2. **Mini:** 2kg-20kg
3. **Small:** 20kg-149kg Cf page 83 **Small unmanned aircraft**
4. **Large:** Above 150kg.

France has the categorisation.

WiFi

WiFi is an internet wireless Local Area Network to IEEE Standard 802.11. It is suitable for the navigation controls of many small drones. Also, it is used for smart devices mounted on drones for applications under the general Internet of Things (IoT) concept, eg for photographs and videos.
See page 9 **Analogue technology**

Wild animals

Australia's University of Adelaide has prepared a precautionary code of best practice for those working near animals for conservation purposes.
The essentials include: a) using a drone and equipment which is non-intrusive, b) keeping the number of flights proportionate to mitigate any disturbance, c) discontinuing work if it proves disruptive, and d) following civil aviation administration rules, and f) following official guidelines for flight and pilot selection.

Wildfires

USA In at least two USA states legislators have or have attempted the introduction of restrictions on drone users flying near wildfires. On several occasions firefighter pilots have had to suspend operations made hazardous by drones.
Canada On a positive note, a Canadian wild fire service is trialling drones which are fitted with thermal imaging technology. The idea is to detect smouldering vegetation in the early cooler morning so that the fire crews are on hand to tackle the problem.
See page 34 **Firefighting**

Will

Making a Will is a personal matter but if the estate is of some size it is essential as a help to the family and executor. Valuable drones and associated protective clothing, equipment and literature would normally be included in the estate and hence in the gross value of the estate.
See page 42 **Inheritance tax liability**

Wind farm turbines

At least one utility's wind turbines are being inspected by a commercial company with drones in much less time than by other methods. With an initial windfarm of 50 or so turbines the service company hopes to develop the service.

Y

yaw

Partial or complete rotation to the left or right around the vertical axis when a drone is flying or hovering; a partial yaw is in effect a change of direction to a new heading.

Z

Zephyr

A solar powered satellite-like military drone used for strategic surveillance from stratospheric heights (circa 65,000 feet). It weighs 30kg and travels at 48km/hr for long periods, eg possibly several months. UK's MOD has four being built, etc.
Pilot recruitment information for Zephyr included the following personal attributes and qualities:

- have or held a manned private pilot's licence or a higher licence
- experience of piloting a UAV or radio controlled model aircraft
- with them, have experience of FPV using standard pilot instruments in a multi-crew situation
- good knowledge of aircraft systems, airmanship, air law, aviation regulations, high altitude meteorology and navigation
- have top-notch a) analytical skills, b) transferable skills, eg interpersonal, verbal and written communications skills
- be able to work with aircrew, customers, employees, and external parties both military and civilian – at all levels.

See page 74 ***peudo-satellite, high altitude***

Abbreviations and Acronyms

The list below:

1. a term defined in the book,
2. a term found in the text of an item but not necessarily defined, and
3. rarely, a term seen in one of the publications listed in Part 3 or elsewhere in drone-related literature.

AAN	Airworthiness Approval Note
ACC	accelerometer
ADDS	Aviation Digital Data Service
ADS-B	automatic dependent surveillance broadcast
AED	automated external defibrillator
AFRL	Air Force Research Laboratory
AGL	above ground level
AMA	Academy of Model Aeronautics
ANO	Air Navigation Order
ARC	Aviation Rulemaking Committee
APPG	All Party Parliamentary Group on Drones
ARF/ARTF	almost ready to fly
ARPAS	Association of Remotely Piloted Aircraft Systems
AUDS	Anti-UAV Defence System
AUVSI	Association for Unmanned Vehicle Systems International
BEC	battery eliminator circuit
B4UFLY	before you fly
BLOS	beyond line of sight
BMFA	British Model Flying Association
BNUC	Basic National UAV Certificate
BNF	ready to be bound
BVLOS	beyond visual line of sight
CAA	Civil Aviation Authority
CAP	Civil Aviation Publication
CCW	Custer wing channel
CF / Cf	carbon fibre / compare
CG	centre of gravity
CIA	Confidentiality, Integrity, and Availability
COA	Certificate of Waiver or Authorisation
CUAV	combat unmanned aviation/aerial vehicle
DDoS	distributed denial of service
DEW	directed energy weapons
DIN	Defence Instructions and Notices
DMA	Defence Manufacture's Alliance
EASA	European Aviation Safety Agency
EO	electro-optic
ERP	Emergency Response Plan
ESC	electronic speed controller
EU	European Union
FAA	Federal Aviation Administration
FAROS	Fireproof Aerial RObot System (FAROS)
FMRA	FAA Modernization and Reform Act 2012
FPV	first person view
GAIL	Gas Authority for India
GPR	ground penetrating radar
GPS	global positioning system
HART	Hazardous Area Response Team
HMRC	Her Majesty's Revenue and Customs
HPC	high-performance computing
HPEC	high-performance embedded computing
IAA	Irish Aviation Authority
ICT	information and communication technology
IEEE	Institute of Electrical and Electronics Engineers
ID Number	identity/registration number
IMU	inertial measurement unit
INS	inertial navigation system

Abbreviations and Acronyms cont.

IR	infrared
ISR	intelligence, surveillance and reconnaissance
JARUS	Joint Authorities for Rule Making on Unmanned Systems
LAMS	Lethal Miniature Aerial Missile Systems
LEO	low-Earth orbit.
LHS	local hobby shop
LiDAR	Light Detection and Ranging
LiPo	lithium polymer battery
LOCUST	Low-Cost Unmanned aerial vehicle Swarming Technology
LOS	line of sight
mAh	milliamp hours
MALE	medium altitude long endurance
MAV	micro air vehicle
MOAS	Migrant Offshore Aid Station
MoD/MOD	Ministry of Defence / modification
MoU	memorandum of understanding
MTCR	Missile Technology Control Regime
mUAS	micro unmanned aircraft systems
NARU	National Ambulance Resilience Unit
NQE	National Qualifying Entity
NOx	nitrogen oxides
ONR	Office of Navy Research
OODA	observe–orient- decide-act
ORS4	Official Record Series 4
PDB	power distribution board
PFAW	permission for aerial work
PIC	pilot in control
Prop	propeller
R&D	Research and Development
RC	radio controlled
RCA	riot control agents
RCAPA	Remote Control Ariel Platform Association
RN	Royal Navy
ROE	rules of engagement
RPAS	remotely piloted aircraft systems
Rpm	revolutions per minute
RSO	remote split operations
RTF	ready to fly
RTH	return to home
RUF	rules for the use of force
Rx	receiver / receive
3s	three cells
S 333	Exemption section 333 giving consent to commercial use of drones
SAA	sense and avoid
SAASM	Selective Availability Anti-Spoofing Module
SDR	special drawing rights
SOP	Standard Operating Procedure
SOx	sulphur oxides
SRG	Safety Regulation Group
SWaP	size, weight and power
Tx	transmitter / transmit
UAS	unmanned aerial system
UAV	unmanned aerial vehicle
UAVS	unmanned aerial vehicle system
UGV	unmanned ground vehicle
UID	unique identification number
UMV	unmanned marine vehicle
USI	Unmanned Safety Institute
USN	United States Navy
USS	United States Ship
UVSA	Unmanned Vehicles Systems Association
UX	user experience
VDP	Vulnerability Disclosure Package
WOT	wide open throttle

Categories of Terms

Agriculture

Agricultural - imagery and analysis
Grants for agriculture and horticulture
Sheep
Spraying with drones
Weed eradication

Airports

Airports and drone threats
Droneport
Exclusion zone
Geofencing
"Inverted wedding cake" poster

Airspace

Airspace-law
Blue line corridor
Exclusion zone
Geofence
"Inverted wedding cake" poster
Red line corridor
Transit zone

Animals

Bird counting
Eagles
Fishing
Hunting and capturing drones
Raptors
Sheep

Commercial and Business

Advantages of working with drones
Business approvals or exemptions
Coal industry
Crowd funding
Developing a service
Electricity grids
Emergency response plan
Energy industry
Exemption under Section 333
Fishing
Forestry operations
Insurance policies
Safety
Standard operating procedure
Warehouse stock control

Components of drones

Accelerometer
Battery eliminator circuit
Boom
Body
Controller
Electronic speed controller
Flight controller
Gimbal
GPS aerial
Gyroscope
Indoor hull
Landing gear
Lithium polymer battery
Power distribution board
Propeller
Rotor
Shell

Connectivity and Telecommunications

Dronecode
Flying a drone and connectivity
Internet connectivity
Internet of Things (IoT)
Internet of Things (IoT) and drones
Standard 802.11
WiFi

Cybersecurity, Data Protection, Security and Surveillance

Airports and drone threats
Auto redaction
CIA (Confidentiality, Integrity, and Availability)
Crowd control
Cybersecurity
Data protection
Data protection principles
Detect and track drones
Drone Information Notice (UK)
Geofence
Hacking
Jamming
Military - Battlefield High Level Persistences Surveillance
National security vetting levels
Police service applications
Police surveillance
Privacy
Protective clothing, equipment, and cybersecurity
Security clearance
Security Cleared Jobs (See page 105)
Selective Availability Anti-Spoofing Module
Spoofing
Surveillance Camera Code of Practice
Surveillance Camera Commissioner

Data Protection See above

Cybersecurity, Data Protection, Security and Surveillance

Deliveries

Blue line Corridor
Cargo drones system
Droneport
Packstation
Red line corridor

Disaster, Emergency Relief and Fire

Ambulance drone
Earthquake relief
Emergency services training
Explosions
Explosion-proof drones
Fire fighting
Fireproof Aerial RObot System (FAROS)
Flooding and drones
Hazards
Smartphone by drone

Drones

Air and sea drone
Ambulance drone
Combat drones
Gremlins Project
Loon Copter
Manufactured Organ Transport Helicopter
Phonedrone
Printable drones
Quadcoptor
Racing drone
Rogue drones
Swarm drone
Telescopic drone
Zephyr

Education and training

Aerial droneology
BNUC
Droneology
Education and training
Emergency services training
Exposition
National Qualifying Entity
Training and assessment

Environments

Finance, Insurance and Taxation

Fire See above **Disaster, Emergency Relief and Fire**

Flying

Health

Insurance See above **Finance, Insurance and Taxation**

Military and Warfare

CICADA
Crowd control
Defense Advanced Research Projects Agency (USA)
Ground control station
Intelligence, surveillance and reconnaissance
Military - Battlefield High Level Persistence Surveillance
Military governance, regulation and UAVSs
Missile Technology Control Regime
Mission - classification of military UAVs
Office of Navy Research (USA)
OODA observe-orient-decide-act
Predator
Remote split operations
Royal Navy and drones (UK)
Rules for the use of force
Rules of engagement (ROE) and drones
Rules of war
Sensors carried by Drones
War Use of Riot Control Agents
Zephyr

Mission See Military and Warfare

Mode See above Flying

Organisations (See Part 6)

Academy of Model Aeronautics (USA)
Association of Remotely Piloted Aircraft Systems (UK)
Aviation Rulemaking Committee (USA)
Civil Aviation Authority (UK)
Defense Advanced Research Projects Agency (USA)
Directorate General of Civil Aviation (India)
Drone Advisory Council (USA)
Drone Manufacturers Alliance
European Aviation Safety Agency (EU)
Federal Aviation Administration (USA)
Lloyds Register (UK)
Missile Technology Control Regime (International)
Office of Navy Research (USA)
Property Drone Consortium (USA)
Rwanda Civil Aviation Authority
South African Civil Aviation Authority
Surveillance Camera Commissioner (UK)
Uganda Aviation Authority
Unmanned Safety Institute (USA)
Unmanned Vehicles Systems Association (USA)

Photography and Filming

Analogue technology
Cameraship
Camera Surveillance – Certification
Filming with drones
Structure from motion (Sfm)
Surveillance Camera Code of Practice
Surveillance Camera Commissioner
Thermal imaging camera
Warp imagery
WiFi

Pilot / Operator

Bind and fly
Daylight operations
First person view (FPV)
Logbook
Operator of a micro drone
PIC
Pilot training
Spotter

Police

Crowd control
Police service applications
Police surveillance

Sea

Air and sea drone
Coastguard – Antarctica sea ice surveillance
Marine applications of drones
Marine nature reserves
Sea ice conditions

Security See above **Cybersecurity, Data Protection, Security and Surveillance**

Sensors See below **Technologies and Sensors**

Standards

European Aviation Safety Agency
EU Standards for drones
Standard 802.11
WiFi

Surveillance See above **Cybersecurity, Data Protection, Security and Surveillance**

Surveying

Digital elevation model
Ordnance Survey plan making
Structure from motion

Technologies and Sensors

Analogue technology
Auto redaction
Brain controlled interface (BCI)
2D-LiDAR sensor
Digital elevation model
Electro-adhesion
Ground penetrating radar
Sensor
Sensors carried by Drones
Structure from motion
Technology applications
Telemetry
Telescopic drones
Warp imagery

Telecommunications See **Connectivity and Telecommunications**

Warfare See **Military and Warfare**

Weather

Gimbal
Glaciers and drone mapping
Meteorology
Weather
Weather forecast

Bibliography and References

Buchan, Philip, (2016)

Eyes in the sky

RICS Land Journal, pp 14-15
Royal Institution of Chartered Surveyors, Parliament Square, London
SW1P 3AD, UK

Bishopstoke Parish Council, (2015)

Byelaws for play areas, public walks, and open spaces,

Bishopstoke Parish Council, Bishopstoke Parish Office, Riverside, Bishopstoke, Eastleigh, Hampshire SO50 6LQ, UK

Boyle, Michael J, (2013, January)

The costs and consequences of drone warfare

International Affairs, Volume 89, Number 1, pp 1-29
John Wiley and Sons Ltd, 9600 Garsington Road, Oxford OX4 2DQ, UK

Cox, Gemma (Editor) (2016, January)

Drone Magazine,

Issue 2, Uncooked Media Ltd, PO Box 6337, Bournemouth, BH1 9EH, UK

Da Vinci, Leonardo, (1505)

Codex on the flight of birds

Copy held at the Royal Library of Turin, Turin, Italy

Edwards, Luke, (2016, April)

Wonders of the drone age

Focus, 34-43, immediate media company, 2nd Floor, Tower House, Fairfax Street, Bristol BS1 3BN

Haysden-Ashby, Camilla, (2016, May/June)

Smarter Farmers

RICS Land Journal, p 15
Royal Institution of Chartered Surveyors, Parliament Square, London SW1P 3AD, UK

Juniper, Adam (2015)

The complete guide to drones

Octopus Publishing Group, Carmelite House, 50 Victoria Embankment, London, EC4Y 0DZ
LaFay, Mark (2015) Drones for dummies
John Wiley & Sons, Inc., 111 River Street, Hoboken, NJ, USA

McCurley, T. Mark with Maurer, Kevin (2015)

Hunter Killer – inside the lethal world of drone warfare,

Allen & Unwin, c/o Atlantic Books, Ormond House, 26-27 Boswell Street, London WC1N 3JZ, UK

Mayer, Michael (2015, July)

The new killer drones: understanding the strategic implications of next-generation unmanned combat aerial vehicles

International Affairs, Volume 91, Number 4, pp 765-780
John Wiley and Sons Ltd, 9600 Garsington Road, Oxford OX4 2DQ, UK

Morison, Jonathan (2016, May 31)

Tiny airport where future is taking off

The Times, p 21
The Times Newspapers Limited, 1 London Bridge Street,
London SE1 9GF, UK

Parsons, Jack (Editor) (2016, No. 005)

Are drones above the law?

Gadget, Volume 5, pp 78-83
Imagine Publishing Limited, Richmond House, 33 Richmond Hill, Bournemouth,
Dorset, BH2 6EZ, UK

Quincey, Duncan and Carrick, Jonathan, (2016, May/June)

Jokulhlaup modelling in Greenland,

RICS Land Journal, pp 12-14
Royal Institution of Chartered Surveyors, Parliament Square,
London SW1P 3AD, UK

Rose, Gideon (Editor) (2015 July /August)

Hi Robot : Fear of flying – Are drones dangerous?

Foreign Affairs, Volume 94, Number 4, pp 177-179
Council on Foreign Relations, 58E. 68th Street, New York, 10065

- Matthews, Robert, **Better safe than sorry** p177 (Comment)
- Johnson, Daniel L, **Written in blood** p178 (Comment)
- West, Gretchen, **West replies**, p179 (Response)

Directory of Organisations

A

Academy of Model Aeronautics (AMA)

A members' group in the USA for individuals who fly model aircraft for recreational and educational purposes; with 120,000 members, it has been in existence for about 80 years. www.modelaircraft.org

Airprox Board, UK

The UK Airprox Board is the investigatory body for UK airspace aviation which looks at the evidence of near-miss events and report findings. It covers hits between aircraft and, increasingly, those in which drones have been involved.

www.airproxboard.org.uk/home/

All Party Parliamentary Group on Drones (APPG)

The APPG on Drones was set up to monitor the use of drones for military and civilian purposes. It covers domestic and international contexts.

www.publications.parliament.uk/pa/cm/cmallparty/register/drones.htm

Assessment and Quality Alliance

The AQA for England, Northern Ireland, and Wales devises A level and AS level qualifications. It is developing an environmental science award which will require studies of the use of UVASs,

www.aqa.org.uk

Association for Unmanned Vehicle Systems International (AUVSI)

With a membership of 7,500 or so, the Association covers a wider field than UAVS, and aims at developing and supporting UAVSs in the civil, commercial, and military groupings.

www.auvsi.org/home

Association of Remotely Piloted Aircraft Systems (UK)

ARPAS (UK) is the principal association for individuals. Membership is open to civilians working in the drone industry in the UK as, for example, pilots, trainers, manufacturers and suppliers. **www.arpas.uk**

Aviation Digital Data Service (ADDS)

A USA FAA-funded package of weather services for the aviation community, eg drone pilots, supported by multi-agency cooperation.

www.aviationweather.gov/adds/

B

British Model Flying Association (BMFA)

Membership organisation, including drone flyers, club events, traning, insurance, etc. Drone aware campaign

www.bmfa.org

British FPV Racing Association (League)

A not-for-profit body of FPV racing pilots which is developing the rapidly growing sport in the UK with a) a set of rules, b) several events later in the year, and c) a website, etc.

www.bfpvrl.org/

C

Civil Aviation Authority (CAA)

The CAA is the UK regulatory body for aviation including unmanned aerial vehicles. Within EU aviation law it is further developing the regime for the regulation of drones in the UK.
www.caa.co.uk/home/

Commercial Drone Alliance

Formally announced on 6 May 2016 the industry-led association's membership includes companies, organisations and associations intent on enhancing the development and growth of the USA commercial drone domain.
www.commercialdronealliance.org/

D

Defense Advanced Research Projects Agency (DARPA)

The Department of Defense (USA) has an agency, DARPA, to research new emerging technologies, eg for UAVS, their application in the military services.
www.darpa.mil/
See Part 2 **Pathfinder Program**

Drone Advisory Council

In the USA, a group set up by the FAA to give advice on drone matters: as: a) development of the drone industry, b) safety, and c) innovation and priority.
www.faa.gov/news/updates/ ?newsId=85528

Dronecode

Dronecode is a not-for-profit association of organisations which is creating a platform for developing software for UVAs by "common shared open sourced" means.
www.dronecode.org/

Drone Defence

A drone technology and security company offering various services to counter intrusive and unwanted drones in commercial and public, etc situations.
www.dronedefence.co.uk/Services

Drone Manufacturers Alliance (DMA)

An organisation formed in April, 2016 by DJI, 3DR, GroPro and Parrott to forward the views of drone manufacturers and their many sector customers to the many national policy makers, particularly in the USA.
www.dronemanufacturersalliance.org/

Drone Pilots Association

An association set up in the USA with the view to representing the interests of small UVA commercial and non-hobbyist pilots.
www.dronepilotsassociation.com

Drone Safe Register (DSR)

A register of qualified commercial pilots (operators) who hold CAA PFW, insurance, etc and are available to hire for one or more drone services in a range of business sectors.
To encourage safer drone flying DSR has a hobbyist section of membership
www.dronesaferegister.org.uk/

E

European Aviation Safety Agency

EASA is the manned aircraft and drone regulation agency for the European Union – particularly for safety standards and drones. Since about 2014 discussions have been conducted into ways in which drones can be brought into Europe's aviation safety regime. These are now within the influences of the Brexit decisions.

www.easa.europa.eu/

F

Federal Aviation Administration

The FAA is the regulatory body for aviation including remotely piloted aircraft (drones) used by for businesses, public services, and recreational and sports enthusiasts in the USA.

www.faa.gov/

FPV UK

FPV UK is the governing body for first person view flying from a recreational perspective.

www.fpvuk.org/

I

Institute of Electrical and Electronic Engineers

Created from two bodies in the USA, it is now a global organisation of over 400,000 engineers, scientists and others furthering technologies and sciences in many fields, eg research, awards, formulating standards, etc.

www.ieee.org/index.html

L

Lloyds Register (LR)

Lloyds Register has prepared guidance notes and case studies for businesses on inspections with unmanned aircraft systems. The notes are part of a research programme concerned with technological matters and technological education for businesses using UAVS and other aspects of technology (See **www.lr.org/en/**)

M

Missile Technology Control Regime (MTCR)

A group of about 34 countries which by association and holding observance of common principles, regulates the export of military grade UAVSs, missiles, and related technology delivery systems. The MTCR covers, for instance, UVASs able to deliver a payload of at least 350 kg to a range of at least 300 km. India joined in 2016.

www.mtcr.info/english/

N

National Aeronautical Centre

The NAC operates out of West Wales Airport and has accommodation and facilities for research and testing UAVSs with the view to developing a knowledge base for national safety standards.It covers the UAV industry for civil, commercial and other purposes. The Centre operates extensive test areas for flying UAVSs over land in Cornwell and Wales and at sea from those areas.

www.nationalaeronauticalcentre.co.uk/

O

Office of Navy Research (ONR)

An establishment of the US Navy which research and tests into drone innovations and technologies are conducted before adoption into use.

www.onr.navy.mil/

P

Professional Society of Drone Journalists

An online international group of about 400 members in nearly 40 countries who follow the code of the association, develop small UAVSs for journalist, etc.
www.dronejournalism.org/

Property Drone Consortium (USA)

Comprised of insurance, roofing, technology and other companies the Property Drone Consortium, to quote:

"... promotes research, development, assessment of regulations and comments on standards for the commercial use of unmanned aircraft systems across the insurance and construction industries. Research focuses on collecting and processing images for inspection and damage detection of building exteriors as well as safety initiatives like collision avoidance and automated flight planning."
www.prweb.com/releases/2016/06/prweb13506641.htm

R

Remote Control Aerial Platform Association (RCAPA)

An association intent on helping members to develop safe flying and safe UAVSs by issuing guidelines, participating with regulatory bodies and others in the industry to improve it for all.
www.rcapa.net/
See Part 2 **Guidelines**

S

Security Cleared Jobs (UK)

The term is the name of a organisation, referred to as a "board", which a) holds a portfolio of jobs requiring security clearance, and b) takes applications from individuals who are cleared or meet the clearance criteria.
www.securityclearedjobs.com

Surveillance Camera Commissioner

For England and Wales a public officer appointed by the Home Secretary under the Protection of Freedoms Act 2012 to carry out the following a) ensure the use of cameras, eg on cameraships, for surveillance is compliant with established principles of usage, b) review the use of cameras for surveillance, c) advise the Home Secretary and others, and d) suggest amendments to policy and practice.
www.gov.uk/government/organisations/surveillance-camera-commissioner

U

Unmanned Vehicles Systems Association (UVSA)

A USA national body comprising local chapters which seeks to educate the public and city government at all levels of UAVs, etc and help members obtain regulatory consents. It also provides a network of industry aspirants.
www.uavs.org/

Unmanned Safety Institute

In the USA, a body developing safety in the drone domains with the intention of creating a global-wide safety culture, eg identifying the "safety gaps" in UAVS industries and plugging them is a priority.
www.unmannedsafetyinstitute.org/

List of Tables

Index of Countries

Short Timeline of Droneology

Introduction

Any attempt at a timeline of "droneology" is likely to be deficient! This lists names, events and developments. It leans heavily on several sources – see Part 6, eg Juniper's excellent book – *"The complete guide to Drones"*.

Year	Names, Events and Developments	Comment
16th Century	Leonardo Da Vinci produced designs of birds, helicopters... - embodying drone-like ideas	At least one has been produced as a working model in modern times
1849	Venice attacked by Austria	Used bombs from balloons
1913	Some success for radio controlled (RC) drone flights	Bellinger flew RC flights using Sperry's recently invented gyroscope
c1930s	Remotely flown drone used	Used to train ack-ack gunners
c1940s	UAVSs used in Europe by USA	Used for a) television ISR and b) bombing – good developmental work but limited success
c1950s	Drones used in Korean War	Used for IRS and combat
1960s-1970s	Drones used in Vietnam war	Numerous ISR flights
1982	Drones used in Syria	Used for ISR and other missions
c1990	Predator in early development	Used for ISR missions
1995	Predator flown in Bosnia	Used for ISR missions
Mid-2010s	Countries start rules and regulations	All over the world dronelaws begin to be written - ongoing
2010	Royal Navy defended a destroyer	Sea Viper missile defence was used to down a target drone.
2013	Taranis flown	Designed as a stealth drone
2014	Trial by DHL for a parcel delivery by drone	Trial was for Juist the North Sea island
2015	Trial by DHL for parcel delivery in Germany	Fully automated Packstations used at Reit im Winkl and on the Winklmoosalm plateau